MAN SWARM

How Overpopulation
is Killing the Wild World

DAVE FOREMAN

WITH LAURA CARROLL

ISBN13: 978-0-9863832-0-5
ISBN10: 0986383201
Jacket design by Creativindie Covers

To Hugh Iltis
A truthteller about
overpopulation and extinction

CONTENTS

FOREWORD

In 2011, I met renowned conservationist Dave Foreman at a population meeting in Washington, D.C. Within days I read the first edition of *Man Swarm* and was inspired by his incredible clarity and courage to speak the truth about overpopulation—human numbers and our impact on the Earth have expanded far above truly sustainable levels and, therefore, must be frozen and then reduced.

That same year, as part of researching her book, *The Baby Matrix*, Laura Carroll contacted me to discuss overpopulation issues. It was not long before *Man Swarm* came up in our discussion.

Laura and I agreed that *Man Swarm* is one of the best books about overpopulation that has been published in the last fifteen years. Originally written largely for conservationists, we wanted this book to reach a wider audience about the perils of overpopulation and population growth. We proposed the development of the second edition of *Man Swarm* to Dave to do just that, and to our delight, he agreed.

Dave Foreman lives and thinks on the cutting edge of conservation issues. Like in the first edition of *Man Swarm*, Dave shows us in this book how he is the bold visionary conservationist and global thinker the world needs to help solve the overpopulation crisis.

Yes, crisis. By the time you finish reading this book, you will understand and we hope you will accept the truths about overpopulation and population growth. Unlike other books on population, you will be armed with ways you can be part of the solution.

We hope you will join us in our deep commitment to solve this issue. If we all act, overpopulation *is* solvable!

David Paxson, President
World Population Balance

INTRODUCTION

WHAT THIS BOOK HOPES TO DO

If true ecological balance exists, then human populations should be stable. They would not grow rapidly for long, nor would they crash.[1]

—Steven LeBlanc

It's painfully straightforward. We have come on like a swarm of locusts, and now at over seven billion and counting, there are too many of us for Earth to harbor. But it is much worse for the other Earthlings—that is, all other living things we share the Earth with—tamed and untamed. A key insight of Charles Darwin's is that all lifekinds can track their beginnings back to a shared forebear. Biologists today call this forebear the Last Common Ancestor or LCA. We—plants, animals, fungi, and microorganisms—are kin. We all share the name, "Earthling."

For many years it has been the booming and spreading overflow of Man that has been the greatest threat to the life of other Earthlings. By Man I mean our species—*Homo sapiens*. I use the word Man in this book as a straightforward way to describe our kind that is not gender specific.

Amongst we Earthlings are "wild things"—or all forms of untamed living things, from plants to wild animals. Aldo Leopold, a top conservation thinker of the twentieth century, wrote in the beginning of his wonderful book, *A Sand County Almanac,* "[T]here are those who can live without wild things, and there are those who cannot." Maybe you are like me; I'm one of those "cannots." I don't want to live in a world without wild things.

In this book, I hope to show you that unless we can freeze and then make Man's footprint on Earth smaller, we will have an Earth with fewer and fewer wild things. I hope to show you that more of our kind means fewer wild things, that a stabilized human population means hope for wild things, and that a shrinking human population means a better world for wild things. And for men, women and children.

It's that straightforward.

In this second edition, my goals for *Man Swarm* are to help readers understand that:

1) the population explosion is ongoing both worldwide and in the United States;

2) the overpopulation of Man is the main driver of the extinction of many kinds of wildlife, the wrecking and taming of wildlands and wild waters, and the creation of pollution, including carbon dioxide and other greenhouse gases;

3) those who do not see a population threat need to be challenged;

4) we will grow to as many as twelve billion in the next one hundred years unless we do something—or unless something awful happens to us, which is likely unless we wake up;

5) there are many things we all can do to freeze and then lower population;

6) overpopulation is solvable!

I hope to give you the background and understanding that inspires you to talk with others about why population stabilization and reduction are so critical in our world today. At the time of this writing, the world population is growing by145 per minute, and the United States has a population of about 314 million. Unless we do something, the population of the United States will double in the next one hundred years to above six hundred million—even up to more than eight hundred million people.

Is this what you want?

What are we going to do about it?

At the first Earth Day in 1970, Hugh Iltis, the great botanist at the University of Wisconsin-Madison (where Leopold also taught), warned that we had begun a mass extinction of other Earthlings. Hugh is one of my mentors and has always taught that our overpopulation drives this mass extinction. This book comes from his trailblazing.

Dave Foreman, 2014

1

MAN'S POPULATION EXPLOSION

The massive growth in the human population through the twentieth century has had more impact on biodiversity than any other single factor.

—*Sir David King,*
science advisor to the British government

Sir David King's words wrap up the last hundred years with the blunt truth—overpopulation is endangering biodiversity, the diversity of plant and animal life in the world.

Complex animal life evolved over five hundred million years ago. Plants came a little later. Half a billion years of geological layers of the Earth show five big extinctions. Each of these big die-offs was brought on by blazing ice balls rocketing through the solar system to hit Earth or the might of geology splitting and moving continents.

Biologists and conservationists call today's extinction, the one that is happening right now—yes, right now—the Sixth Mass Extinction. This one stands alone. It's been brought on willfully by one kind of life form warring against all others.[1] Today's Sixth Mass Extinction boils down to one species.

Homo sapiens.

Us.

Never before has one kind of being become such a mighty swarm, spreading over Earth to almost everywhere and scalping forests, grasslands, deserts, and other wildlands in its wake.

Never before has one kind of life gobbled up so much of all other forms of life and what they need to live.

And never before have so few become so many so fast—with billions now standing where thousands once stood.

For every *Homo sapiens* alive fifty thousand years ago, there are one million alive today.

We have flooded the Earth with ourselves.

POPULATION GROWTH MAN 50KYA TO 2050 C.E.

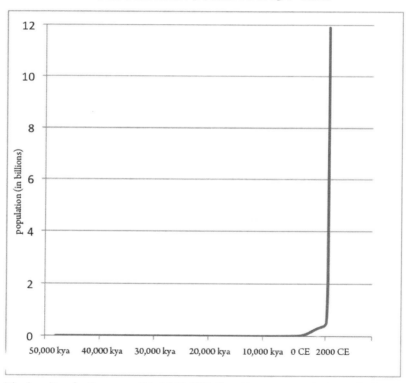

The baseline for "years ago" is 2000 C.E. So 10kya is 8,000 B.C.E. The beginning of the Current Era (C.E.) is 2kya (two thousand years ago). Sources include the United Nations Population Division and the Bixby Center, University of California, San Francisco.

An Unforgivable Outcome of Population Explosion

Unlike most books that warn of overpopulation, in this book I spend little time on tales about coming starvation, breakdown of civilizations, running out of oil, and wars and anarchy over dwindling raw goods. It's not because I downplay or reject these likelihoods, but because the most dreadful and unforgivable outcome of our human population explosion is what we are doing to all other forms of life on Earth. And this isn't something that might happen in years to come; it is happening right now.

Most people who have written about overpopulation have underplayed and overlooked the way our growth drives the end of other forms of life. Many people are aware of this population wound. However, when I give talks I find there are always some people in the crowd who ask how we can hope to keep or rebuild wilderness and wildlife if we don't halt population growth. More and more people are realizing that without freezing human numbers, we can't keep our national parks, stop the loss of polar bears and elephants and whales, and we can't hope to put the brakes on greenhouse gases to halt irreparable climatic damage.

The Population Explosion in a Nutshell

Sixty-five thousand years seems like forever, yet it is a finger-snap in geological time. Walk with me back to that time. In east and southeast Asia, there were more than ten kinds (species[2]) of great apes, two kinds of orangutans, and two or more kinds of *Homo erectus* offspring. There were tiny little folks (yes, real hobbits) on Flores and other islands. In Africa there were two kinds of gorillas, chimpanzees and bonobos, and likely two hominin kinds, one of which was becoming us—*Homo sapiens*. In Europe and western Asia, there were Neandertals.[3] In central Asia, there was also another kind of *Homo* which was not us and not Neandertal. Of the great ape species, who do you think was fewest?

It was likely our forebears. Genetic and other scientific work shows that there were fewer than ten thousand of the elder *Homo sapiens* living sixty-five thousand years ago—maybe only five thousand.[4] Fifty thousand years later, we had spread out of Africa to Asia, Australia, Europe, and the Americas. Only Antarctica and a few out-of-the-way islands were yet without us.[5] In a few more thousand years we were building yearlong settlements and starting to grow wheat and lentils. We had already brought some wolves into our packs and would soon tame goats and sheep. And some little desert cats would tame us. About ten thousand years ago, our tally had climbed to a million or so. By that time, our nearest kin—the three to six other *Homos*—were gone, and we likely had much to do with their going. The Sixth Mass Extinction was going full tilt with our killing of the biggest kinds of wildlife around at the time, like seven-ton woolly mammoths.[6]

Another way to look at it is that fifty thousand years ago there were more tigers than *Homo sapiens*—more gorillas, more chimpanzees, more orangutans, more blue whales, more jaguars, and more white rhinos. Today, for every wild tiger on Earth, there are *two million* human beings. Close your eyes for a minute and think about that.

One hundred years ago, in India alone, there were some one hundred thousand tigers in the wild. As the human population shot through the roof in India, the population of tigers fell through the floor.

Then tackle this one—today, about three hundred sixty thousand babies are born every day. This is more than the total population of all the other great apes (gorillas, chimpanzees, bonobos, and orangutans) put together.[7]

MAN AND TIGER POPULATION IN INDIA, 1900-2025 C.E.

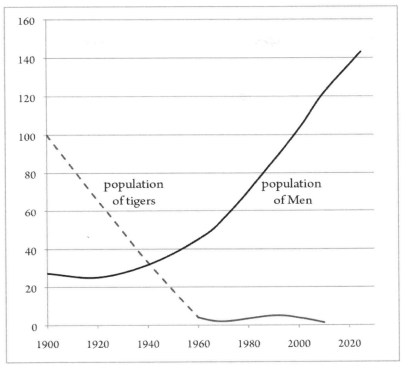

The vertical axis shows the population of tigers in thousands, and it shows the population of Man in tens of millions. One hundred thousand tigers correspond to one billion men. The source for Man is the United Nations Population Division.

Father-son historians William and J. R. McNeill write, "By the time the first metropolitan web was forming around Sumer (Mesopotamia, or southern Iraq) some five thousand years ago, the earth hosted perhaps ten to thirty million people."[8] The widely acknowledged world population when AD time began was two hundred fifty million. By 1700 AD, about the time Benjamin Franklin was born, we had grown to 610 million. Throughout this time of preindustrial civilization, heavy childhood deaths, epidemics, and wars slowed growth.[9]

Man Population Growth from 0-2050 C.E.

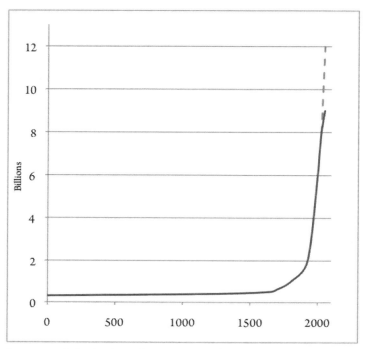

Sources include the United Nations Population Division and the Bixby Center, University of California, San Francisco.

So:

65,000 years ago we were less than 10,000

10,000 years ago: 1,000,000

5,000 years ago: 10,000,000 to 30,000,000

2,000 years ago: 250,000,000

300 years ago: 610,000,000

Our population grew sturdily, but pretty slowly and over many, many years. Soon, however, our population growth was to *explode*.

In 1999, physician and University of Colorado anthropology professor Warren Hern wrote:

"People who are forty years old or more in 1998 are among the first people in history to have lived through a doubling of

18

Man Population Growth by Billions, 1804-2050 C.E.

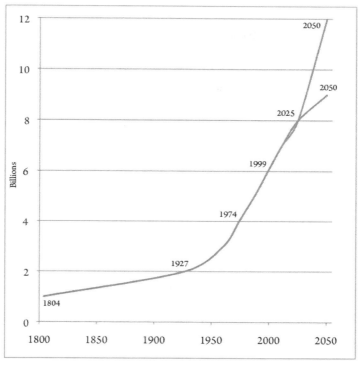

This graph uses the same sources as the previous graph, and shows Man's growth by billions, from 1 billion in 1804 on.

world population; people who are seventy-five years old have seen the human population triple."[10]

I was born in 1946 and have now seen the world population triple in my lifetime from about two billion to over seven billion. My father-in-law, Robert Morton, born in 1912, saw world population more than quadruple in his ninety-nine years.

This warning from Warren Hern ought to jar your mind:

Man's population grew more in the last forty years than in the previous three million.[11]

This is why we talk about the human population *explosion*.

It's About Overpopulation, Not Population Growth

No one would disagree that our population has grown since 1700. The same goes for the numbers that reflect the exponential growth curve of human population. Where the clash comes is with forecasts, with one camp saying that population growth is slowing, even as they say such growth is not a worry. Some of the wrangle comes from the handful of ways to calculate population growth, including rate of growth, whether the rate of growth itself is going up or down (and by what speed), how many hungry mouths are added each year, the number of women coming into their baby-making years, population doubling time, and so on.

Biologist and ecologist Garrett Hardin laid out why we need to look at all these kinds of population growth. Say that the *percentage rate* of growth slows from 2.1 percent to 1.7 percent a year over a few years while the *absolute increase* of yearly growth goes from sixty-four million to seventy-nine million to ninety-three million in that time. How can this be? *Because there are more women giving birth at the lower rate.*

Hardin wrote in 1993, "The absolute rate of increase has increased every year since the end of World War II. It is the absolute increase, rather than the relative rate, that stresses the environment."[12] In terms of absolute increases, there are some seventy-five million more hungry people in 2013 than in 2012.

Another way to look at population is by population age structure. Even if there is a drop in a nation's growth rate, its population still *rises* for many years. Why? As big segments of the population go through their childbearing years, they have many, many children. In 1995, one-third of Earth's population (two billion) was under fifteen years of age, while only about five percent of it (three hundred million people) was over sixty-five. The youngsters are making far more babies now than the number of oldsters that are dying; therefore, the population is growing.[13]

Latest population numbers show lopsided percentages under fifteen years old. With such a landslide of youngsters coming into their childbearing years, even if we reduce birth rates to the replacement level of 2.1 children per woman, it will take two or three generations, or fifty to seventy-five years, before the population stabilizes.[14] In many African countries today, between forty and fifty percent of the population is under fifteen years of age. With that lopsidedness, forecasts for growth in these lands are unbearable.

And here is another twist. Population does not grow evenly over the world. While Italy, Japan, and Russia may have ended their growth, elsewhere—Africa foremost—growth is *unbelievably high*. Take Ethiopia, where there is rampant hunger. As this graph shows, it had fewer than nineteen million souls in 1950,

ETHIOPIA POPULATION GROWTH, 1950-2050 C.E.

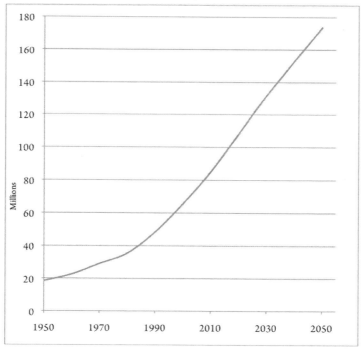

Source: United Nations Population Division: World Population prospects: 2008 Revision, Medium variant as of Feb. 18, 2011.

forty million or so when it had its 1984 famine, eighty-five million today, and is slated to have about 174 million in another forty years.

I find it hard to believe that Ethiopia can grow to 174 million folks by 2040. How on Earth can this happen? I don't mean how can we let it happen, I mean how is it biologically, physically possible for it to happen?

J. Kenneth Smail, Professor Emeritus of Anthropology at Kenyon College, speaks to another piece of the puzzle that's mostly overlooked. "Ongoing global gains in human longevity will continue to make a major contribution to world population expansion over the next half-century, *regardless of whatever progress might be made in reducing fertility* (my emphasis)."[15] In other words, how longevity grows population is a big deal.

In the 1960s and 1970s, population biologists like Paul Ehrlich and ecologists like Garrett Hardin woke up governments and the public with their warnings. Birth control of all kinds became widespread in the 1970s. Good work was done—at least for a while. But in no way has the population bomb been defused. If you count births minus deaths, we add some eighty million more mouths to feed every year. That's eight hundred million every ten years.

Go back a few pages. Just three hundred years ago, we were six hundred ten million. We are adding more than that every ten years. Don't believe those foisting tales that the population bomb has fizzled. Human population has exploded gruesomely in the last two hundred years. And it will keep shooting up for some time.

How high will the world population go? In 2011, we hit seven billion, and there was naïve talk about leveling off at eight billion by 2050 without much explanation about how this will happen. Recent projections say about 9.6 billion and continue to climb. But Dr. Joseph Speidel of the University of California's

Bixby Center for Reproductive Health Research & Policy warns, "If birth rates remain unchanged, world population will grow to 11.9 billion by 2050."[16] The "official" projections of 9.6 billion by 2050 are grounded, then, in the belief that birth rates will somehow reduce. But will they without a dedicated effort for fewer births? Or will they go down as a result of something awful?

2

THE GREAT SHORTSIGHTEDNESS

It is critical to focus on what is presently dead certain: that overproduction and overpopulation have been driving the dismantling of complex ecosystems and native life, and leaving in their widening wake constructed environments, simplified ecologies, and lost life forms.

—*Eileen Crist*

In the 1960s and 1970s, snipping the wires on the population bomb was high on the lists of conservationists and environmentalists. But over forty years and over two *billion* more mouths later, most shy away from hard talk on population growth. As Roy Beck and Leon Kolankiewicz wrote in the *Journal of Policy History*, "As [the modern environmental] movement enters its fourth decade, perhaps the most striking change is the virtual abandonment by national environmental groups of U.S. population stabilization as an actively pursued goal."[1]

Given the long history of worry about limits to population growth, this step back is all the more upsetting. In 1968, population biologist and Stanford University professor Paul Ehrlich and his wife Anne Ehrlich authored the book *The Population Bomb*, which became a best seller. They also wrote *Population Resources Environment*, which went into academic depth on everything from erosion and pollution to birth control.[2] These books and others helped me learn that Man's population growth was at the root of nearly every wildland woe—such as coal strip-mines, dams on wild rivers, and new roads in the National Forest back-country, all of which I was fighting at the time. Then and now, we can weigh the strength of conservation groups on overpopulation by the steps they take:

- ❖ Do they acknowledge the threat?
- ❖ Do they acknowledge overpopulation as the driver of extinction and other ecological wounds?
- ❖ Do they teach it?
- ❖ How tough are they on the plight?
- ❖ Do they call for freezing population or, better yet, lowering it?
- ❖ Do they stand behind the kinds of steps that are needed?

With the exception of *Wild Earth* magazine and The Wildlands Project in the 1990s and early 2000s, in recent times you will be hard pressed to find a mainstream national conservation group that is straightforward and forthright on overpopulation. As long as Senator Gaylord Nelson, "the Father of Earth Day," was alive, The Wilderness Society (for which he worked after his Senate career) was steadfast on population. With his passing, however, The Wilderness Society seems to have dropped it like a hot po-tato. The same goes for local and regional organizations. Even the Sierra Club—which was involved in the publishing of *The Population Bomb*—has become wittingly weak-kneed about it.

Caring about worldwide overpopulation is also shunned outside the conservation clan. Those who write about and who are harmed by the outcomes of overpopulation can also be blind to what is behind their many plights. Take the article in *The New York Times* about hunger and the lack of wild food for a tribe in

THE GREAT SHORTSIGHTEDNESS

the Amazon that shows off Chief Kotok of the Kamayura. The reporter writes about the once-many fish no longer being there and how Kotok's "once-idyllic existence had turned into a kind of bad dream." He is "stressed and anxious" about how to care for his twenty-four children.[3] Did you catch that? It seems that neither Chief Kotok nor the *Times* reporter did. Might having twenty-four children have anything to do with there being fewer fish in the river and less game in the jungle?

Another article in the *Times* tells about a wailing farmer in Syria who has been wiped out by not being able to feed his family. He has two wives and *fifteen* children.[4] I could go on with such tales. In today's world we are beset with woes right and left, most of which come from or are made worse by growth, yet it is taboo to even whisper that growth of the Man swarm might have something to do it.

The big question for lovers of wild things is the one that Garrett Hardin threw at us back in 1972: "[H]ow do we get the general body politic to accept the truth?"[5] We must also ask, "How do we get today's conservationists and environmentalists to accept the truth?"

Over the last two hundred years, some of the world's most farsighted thinkers have warned about human overpopulation. From their writings we can tease out five threads that result from population growth and overpopulation:

1) Hunger and starvation because we can't grow enough to feed ourselves;
2) Squandering natural resources (raw goods) until we run out;
3) Landscalping and the loss of land fertility;
4) Cultural, economic, and political upheaval; and
5) Harm to wild things.

27

Most of those who want limits to growth worry most about the first four—after all, they are about us. Far fewer give heed to how our growth gobbles up ecosystems and drives to extinction a swelling stream of species each year—soon to be an overwhelming flood.

The Crucial Question

The crusty philosophy professor and High Sierra climber George Sessions wrote, "One's position on the human overpopulation issue serves as a litmus test for the extent of one's ecological understanding and commitment to protecting biodiversity and the integrity of the Earth's ecosystems."[6] He does not say anything about running out of food or oil; he speaks for wild things.

Like Sessions, Professor Eileen Crist at Virginia Tech is an unclouded thinker on population stabilization. Her 2003 essay in *Wild Earth,* "Limits-to-Growth and the Biodiversity Crisis," outlines a landmark population stabilization strategy. While most who warn about population growth talk about how booming numbers will lead to not being able to feed ourselves, running out of oil, water, and other must-needs, Crist sees two weaknesses with this path: (1) "Limits-to-growth proponents cannot predict exactly when, or how, industrial civilization" will overshoot natural limits and crash; and (2) "In crucial ways, the debate between the limits-to-growth and pro-growth proponents is extraneous to the ecological crisis, especially to the plight of nonhumans; and it constitutes a digression."[7] She also writes:

> *The core issue is not the quandary of real-world limits but what kind of real world we desire to live in…It is critical to focus on what is presently dead certain: that overproduction and overpopulation have been driving the dismantling of complex ecosystems and native life, and leaving in their*

widening wake constructed environments, simplified ecolo-
gies, and lost life forms.[8]

She asks, "Does the framework of 'breaching limits' <on growth> address the momentous event of the biodiversity crisis? Arguably, it does not. It is perfectly possible that a mass extinction of fifty percent, sixty percent, or more of the Earth's species would not be pragmatically catastrophic for human beings."[9] You only need to look at some of the most heavily settled and domesticated lands, such as the British Isles and northwestern Europe, to see how life can be fat and full for Man with few wild animals and little or no land with its native vegetation. These kinds of cultivated lands can be productive for Man for many years.

Leaders of mainstream conservation and environmental groups have been shortsighted in not acknowledging that whenever the needs of Man come up against the needs of wildlife, it is wildlife that loses. In a nation and a world with a growing population, wildlife will lose over the long haul.

Crist so rightly asks, "The crucial question, then, is not whether a colonized world is viable but rather: Who…wants to live in such a world?" She holds that we need "to be as clear and precise as possible about the consequences of the humanized order under construction: in this emerging reality it is not our survival and well-being that are primarily on the line, but *everybody else's*."[10]

The outcomes of Man's growth yesterday, today, and tomorrow have resulted in scalped wildlands, endangered and extinct wildlife, and sweeping climatic upset. These awful upshots are what lovers of wild things should bring up when we talk about growth. We lovers of wild things need to talk about the inborn worth of wild things and how it is a sin for Man to shove them off into the pit of extinction.

Our mad dash to grow more food and to suck out oil and gas in faraway spots is what has led to the landscalping that drives the landslide of extinction. At the 2005 meeting of the American Geophysical Union in San Francisco, researchers from the University of Wisconsin-Madison showed that since 1700, "the amount of cultivated land on the planet has increased from seven to forty percent."[11] In the last three hundred years, then, one-third of Earth's wildlands have been tamed and chopped up into crop fields. One-third of Earth's land has had wild trees, shrubs, and grasses torn out and crops planted instead. Conservation biologist Reed Noss has thoroughly tallied the loss of sundry ecosystems in the United States. There are once-sprawling wild neighborhoods such as Tallgrass Prairie, Southeastern Canebrakes, and Longleaf Pine Forests that hardly exist anymore.[12]

To put this in perspective:

All of this has happened since Benjamin Franklin was born (1706).

Most of this has happened since Abraham Lincoln was born (1809).

Throughout the earlier ten thousand years of farming, only seven percent, or one out of every fourteen acres, of landed Earth was tamed by our crops. Now this happens to be forty percent, or *two out of every five acres*. No wonder thousands of species have been lost, and it is bound to happen to thousands more.

3

REDEFINING CARRYING CAPACITY

The cumulative biotic potential of the human species exceeds the carrying capacity of its habitat.

—*William Catton, Jr.*

In 1944, a handful of reindeer were set loose on St. Matthew Island in the Bering Sea off Alaska. Although this 128-square-mile island had good habitat, neither reindeer nor their kin caribou had been there earlier. Also missing were hunters of the reindeer—gray wolves. From the first twenty-nine animals, the population boomed to six thousand in nineteen years. The herd crashed to only forty-two reindeer three years later.[1]

What happened? The reindeer overpopulated their home and ate up their island. Thanks to the widespread myth of human exceptionalism, most people think this kind of tale won't happen to Man. We are not thralls to biology, like animals. We are a kind alone.

But an unsettling saga that happened on Henderson Island, one of the most out-of-the-way dots in the South Pacific, tells a different story. A European ship first stumbled upon it in 1606. No one lived there then. It seemed that no one had ever lived there. Henderson's lack of Man settlement had to be rethought in the 1980s when bird paleontologists Storrs Olson and David

Steadman found the bones of three extinct species of pigeons and three extinct species of seabirds on the island. Only after they dug up the bones did they find Polynesian archaeological sites. Man *had lived* on Henderson, hunted native birds to extinction, and then died out themselves or left. As author Jared Diamond writes, "Given the widespread evidence for overexploitation of wild animals by early Polynesians, not only Henderson but the other mystery islands as well may represent the graveyards of human populations that ruined their own resource base."[2]

The nightmare we are up against today is whether we can keep from turning Earth into Henderson Island. Unless we can cut back our own breeding, Henderson may be our tomorrow. And we will do to the wildlife of Earth what the Polynesians did to the wildlife of Henderson.

The sagas on St. Matthew Island and Henderson Island involve a key yardstick in ecology called the "carrying capacity" of the ecosystem for each species. Think of an animal—let's say the mule deer. Determining its carrying capacity means knowing how many an area can "carry" without harm to the ecosystem or starvation of those deer. Biologists know what it means for Earthlings other than us. But what about the carrying capacity for Man? Professor Eileen Crist at Virginia Tech wisely writes, "In most of the literature I've read raising the question of 'what human carrying capacity is' seems to be a veiled way of asking: How many people can sustainably use, exploit, degrade, or destroy (portions of) the biosphere without risking collapse for human beings or human civilization?"[3]

All too often, carrying capacity is weighed narrowly and focuses on whether Earth can give mankind what it needs. And all too often, it overlooks the needs of all other Earthlings; wild things do not play into this reckoning. Beyond its impact on the flow of raw goods in our industrial web, it is past time for carrying capacity to include its impact on wild things and on evolutionary processes.

The Unending Saga

Two hundred years ago, an early English economist named Thomas Malthus wrote, "Population, when unchecked, increases in a geometrical ratio. Subsistence increases only in an arithmetical ratio." But what does this mean ecologically? William Catton, Jr., author of *Overshoot*, writes:

> *Throughout the essay Malthus was referring to human population, and by subsistence he meant food...these conceptions were unduly narrow. But the really basic Malthusian principle is so important that it needs to be restated in the more accurate vocabulary of modern ecology. It states a relationship of inequality between two variables: The cumulative biotic potential of the human species exceeds the carrying capacity of its habitat.[4]*

What is the bedrock biological truth? There are limits, and we can overshoot them. It is the way things are—like gravity.

Malthus' thinking influenced Charles Darwin to see natural selection as a key tool in evolution. Restated in the ecological language of today, what Darwin spun out of Malthus was—the cumulative biotic potential of *any* species exceeds the carrying capacity of its habitat.

So, within a species, each will struggle with each for short goods. Some will be better than others in that scrap. The more fit ones will more often live to breed and hand on their winning genes; the less fit ones will often die before they breed, or will rear fewer offspring.[5] Two English naturalists half a world away from each other—Charles Darwin in England and Alfred Russel Wallace in the Dutch East Indies—grasped that this was the main way one kind of being evolved into another or into many—*natural selection.*

Archaeologist Steven LeBlanc brings this core biological thought to bear for understanding the prehistory and history of Man in his myth-smashing book *Constant Battles*. Whether in bands or empires, we have fought with our neighbors as far back as our kind goes. The saga plays out like this:

> Population grows
> Carrying capacity is overshot
> Hunger and starvation step in
> You fight your neighbors for what they have
> Such fighting cuts population
> And the game begins anew

Overshooting carrying capacity has always been part of this repeating cycle.

The Age of Exuberance

Five hundred years ago, we opened an age of exuberance with Columbus' westward sailings. Before that, Europe was crowded and raw goods were short. There were only twenty-four acres of land for each European. With the finding and exploitation of the New World, however, there were now one hundred twenty acres of land per person. This rocked the way Europeans had seen the world. As Catton says, "The new premise of limitlessness spawned new beliefs, new human relationships, and new behavior."[6] English settlers in North America in the 1600s were so overawed by the wealth of the new land that they hatched the myth of "superabundance"—the mainspring for the westward movement and the careless and uncaring scalping of the land for about the next three hundred years.

However, the New World was not empty of us when Europeans "discovered" it. Nor were Australia and New Zealand.

Many tribes, chiefdoms, and kingdoms already dwelt in these vast landscapes, though most often not densely. Europe took over these lands and brought down or killed the people already there (with great help from illnesses brought by Europeans, for which those in the Americas, Oceania, Australia, and New Zealand had no immunity).[7]

Takeover did not begin in 1500 though. As I wrote in *Rewilding North America*, we *Homo sapiens* have been taking over lands for at least forty thousand years from other species of hominins.[8] In those forty thousand years, bands of *Homo sapiens* have been taking over lands from other bands of *Homo sapiens,* first in Africa and Eurasia and then in Australia, the Americas, Oceania, and New Zealand. For the last ten thousand years, farmers have been taking over land ever more fully from hunter-gatherers and other farmers. But never before had a literate civilization taken over a whole new world as Europeans did with the Americas.[9]

"About two hundred years ago," writes Catton, "carrying capacity was tremendously (but temporarily) augmented by a quite different method; takeover gave way to drawdown." An agrarian economy became an industrial economy through the exploitation of fossil fuels. Coal, oil, and natural gas made the agricultural yield boom, through fertilizers and pesticides made from them and machinery fueled by them (which also freed up one-quarter to one-third of all cropland from growing feed for draft horses and oxen).

On the heels of the fossil fuel breakthrough came another—death control. Scientific medicine, with germ theory leading to curbing infection, public health work, and then to antibiotics and vaccinations, deeply cut baby and childbirth deaths, and the human population grew even faster.[10] Thanks to scientific medicine, old ills were not as deadly as they once had been, and more people began to live longer. When people live longer, it boosts population growth because more people are alive at one time.

Carrying Capacity & Net Primary Production

What sets the carrying capacity of a landscape? It's the resource that will run out the soonest. If iron, timber, clean air, land, and oil are overflowing but a country runs out of water, it has overshot carrying capacity.[11] What seems to have run out first for industrial Man is the ability of the atmosphere and the oceans to hold our greenhouse gases. We haven't thought of such waste "sequestration" and other "ecosystem services" as resources or raw goods like coal and timber before, but mark my words, we will.

Looking at carrying capacity in terms of resources thinks only of Man. The true yardstick of our carrying capacity should go beyond how ecosystems serve us to what we do to wild things—the health and soundness of other Earthlings and where they live. A landscape without big wilderness and without room for wild animals and native wildlife is one in which humans have overshot carrying capacity. Defining carrying capacity in this way means humans overshot it in much of the world long ago.

What "sustainability" means has also been seen through the lens of Man's needs. A society is not truly sustainable if it brings on extinction of other Earthlings or if it tames its lands and waters. It is unlikely that any tribe has been sustainable for long even for its own needs alone. Truly defining sustainability and figuring out what we must do to gain it is the great challenge of all time for Man.

Meanwhile Man lords over Earth. How much we hold sway is shown by the ecological yardstick called net primary production (NPP). As Paul and Anne Ehrlich write, NPP is "all the solar energy annually captured worldwide by photosynthesizers and not used by them to run their own lives." NPP is what makes biomass. Ecologist Stuart Pimm writes, "Biomass is how much living stuff the planet has. Production is how much new stuff grows each year—the products of photosynthesis."[12] In 1986, in one way or another Man was taking about forty percent of the terrestrial NPP of our world, or twenty-five percent when the ocean NPP was brought in.[13] According to Pimm, we are gobbling up forty-two percent of terrestrial NPP, and we are taking "a quarter to a third of the oceans' production."[14] Catton warns, "Such total exploitation of an ecosystem by one dominant species has seldom happened, except among species which bloom and crash…Having become a species of superdetritovores, mankind [is] destined not merely for succession, but for crash."[15]

Reg Morrison, author of *The Spirit in the Gene,* calls us a "plague species," and the truth is we will be unless we can do what we have never done before—hold back the number of us on the planet.[16] To do this we must redefine carrying capacity, ecological footprints, and sustainability to include all Earthlings. We need to starkly recognize that overshooting this carrying capacity will lead us to join a sweep of cultures from the last ten thousand years and set ourselves up for crash.

4

HOW THE MAN SWARM
EATS THE EARTH

Except for giant meteorite strikes or other such catastrophes,
Earth has never experienced anything like the contemporary
human juggernaut. We are in a bottleneck of overpopulation
and wasteful consumption that could push half of Earth's
species to extinction in this century.[1]

—*E. O. Wilson*

In its article "Owning Up to Overpopulation," the Center for Biological Diversity says flatly, "Today, overpopulation is at the root of virtually all threats to species around the globe."[2] There are five stacks of woe that our Man swarm brings: (1) Landscalping, (2) Resource depletion, (3) Starvation, (4) Social, political upheaval, and (5) Ecological/Evolutionary wounds.

By landscalping, I literally mean the "scalping" of land. The scythe of civilization wipes out the homes of wildlife, wrecks watersheds, and thereby fouls streams, rivers, silts in lakes and ocean estuaries. It withers and shrivels ecosystems.

Depleting resources, or draining raw goods until there is little left, leads to scrambling to get whatever is left in still-wild places and then to ripping it out in hasty, careless ways. When gasoline prices shot up in the United States in 2008, polls showed growing backing for drilling offshore and in the Arctic National Wildlife Refuge. Chants of "drill, baby, drill" in the 2008 presidential campaign were hotheaded marks of feared resource scantiness. Wild things then pay with the blowout of BP's deep-ocean well in the Gulf of Mexico.

Food shortages are the worst dearth for Man. Hungry women, children, and men become refugees crowding into wherever they think they might find food and thereby trampling and ransacking healthier lands. In a world of tabloid-television news, heartbreaking tales of starving mothers and children lead to calls to jump up food-growing elsewhere, which then leads to the stripping and withering of wildlands not good for long-time cropping. More irrigation dams throughout the world will be another upshot of starvation brought on not by too little food but by too many mouths.

Author and environmental analyst Lester Brown sees water shortages as one of the worst things over the hill. Some seventy percent of the world's freshwater now goes into irrigating crops. Groundwater is being sucked out by irrigation wells and is dropping ever lower, so wells have to be drilled deeper.[3] When this happens, springs dry up. Rivers and streams run to cracked mud and blowing dust. Without trusty old watering holes, wildlife of all kinds is shoved to the edge, has to leave, or dies. The freshwater upheaval rooted in the Man swarm is not only a threat to Man, it is even more of a threat to thousands of kinds of other Earthlings.

Brown brings up a spooky statistic, "175 million Indians consume grain produced with water from irrigation wells that will soon be exhausted."[4] What will those 175 million (or, perhaps, 275 million, given India's ongoing growth) do when the water and the grain run out? What will they do to the land and to wildlife living nearby? Where will they go? How much weight will there be on the Indian government to "open" land now in national parks and other tiger havens?

Where millions on the edge have overshot carrying capacity and now are starving, then food aid is rushed in, we can be sure of one thing. When deadly hunger hits that land again in twenty years, there will be twice as many empty bellies as before, making more wretchedness and hunger down the trail, unless that aid comes with hard-nosed, unyielding birth-control goals. Without an end to population growth in India, the homes of what wild animals are left will also be ransacked.

Besides starvation, social breakdown brought on by too many young men could lead to hordes doing their utmost to take over less-crowded, wealthier lands. Food-energy-hope-starved countries will make war on one another, and when they do, wild things will often be the great losers. Some Hutus in Rwanda truthfully acknowledged that overcrowding was behind their slaughter of Tutsis; they wanted their land for themselves and their children. Thanks to overpopulation, look for much more of this tribal killing within "nations" as everything gets tighter.

Now let's look at how overpopulation is behind ecological and evolutionary woes.

The Seven Ecological Wounds

There are seven ways overpopulation harms the wild world. I call them the *Seven Ecological Wounds*.

Wound 1: Overkill

When I was young I learned how the "harvesting" of the seven seas would feed more and more people. We've done that, but what has happened? The crashing of fisheries throughout the world, the die-off of coral reefs, and the functional extinction of keystone species such as cod, sharks, and tuna.

41

As hungry little settlements swell and spread out, they gobble up the bigger wildlife from rainforests and other wildlands. Even a little knot of huts with near-Stone-Age tools can clean out the bigger wildlife in a nearby protected area. As more babies grow up and become parents, hunters have to go ever farther afield. Historically, hunting has caused the global extinction, local extirpation, or near-extinction of wildlife, including once-highly abundant bison, passenger pigeons, shorebirds, whales, cod, elephants, sea turtles, and many more. Such hunting has been driven by the "need" for meat and new settlements and cropland by ever-growing populations of people worldwide and locally.

Wound 2: Scalping and Taming Wilderness

Although direct killing is still fulsome in much of the world, it has become less of a threat in the United States. Here, ransacking and taming wildlands may do even more harm than the other wounds. The growing Man swarm in the U.S. is the leading driver for scalping neighborhoods lived in by wild things and remaking them into new neighborhoods for men, women, and children. Philip Cafaro and Winthrop Staples write, "Between 1982 and 2001, the United States converted thirty-four million acres of forest, cropland, and pasture to developed uses, an area the size of Illinois." The acreage cleared, paved, built on, and otherwise remade for Man has also been going up since 1982, from 1.4 million acres to 2.2 million acres every year. And bulldozers continue to eat more acres every year.[5]

Crop fields and heavily grazed pastures are no better and sometimes even worse for wildlife than towns are. But when farms and ranches are pimpled with homes, streets, and strip malls, their food-growing acreage has to be made up for elsewhere by plowing wildland or by more irrigation, fertilizers, and pesticides on less giving land. Some of the richest cropland in California and elsewhere in the U.S. has been lost to sprawl.

The building of bigger homes and the shift from the Rustbelt to the Sunbelt speed the cancerous sprawl of suburban and exurban bedroom neighborhoods in the U.S. But the growing population in the U.S. is an even bigger driver of sprawl. More mouths lead to more acres of wildland scalped for cropland, too. Recall that University of Wisconsin researchers say "the amount of cultivated land on the planet has increased from seven to forty percent" since 1700.[6] In about three hundred years, the acres needed to feed Man have gone from less than ten percent to nearly half of Earth's land acres—more than a *fivefold* rise.

Spin a globe. One-third of what you see that is not water or ice has gone from neighborhoods for wildlife to food lands for Man in just three hundred years—which is only three percent of the time since full-on agriculture began and less than one percent of the time since *Homo sapiens* crossed the Red Sea out of Africa. This mind-numbing, heartbreaking wreckage of the wild is the main driver for the extinction of heaps of beings worldwide and the nosedive of others, like butterflies, elephants, and tigers.

In India, leapfrogging growth of tribal folk today is nibbling away at tiger reserves. New laws are afoot to let tribals settle in once well-shielded wildlands that have been the last havens for tigers and other animals. Indian conservationists worry that tigers will not last long where this happens. Coomi Kapoor warns that the decline of tigers in India comes from the "pressure of human population, especially tribal groups."[7] In India, Bangladesh, Sumatra, and elsewhere in Asia, when booming crowds overrun wildlands, clashes with tigers and elephants grow, and big cats and tuskers die. Likewise, when Americans shove new houses, yards, and streets into wildlands, we hear more and more griping to "control" cougars, coyotes, and other wildlife that were living there long before we moved in.

Norman Myers, the British biologist who may have been the first to warn that we were in a mass extinction, has looked at overpopulation and biodiversity "hotspots." Hotspots, as described by some international conservation groups, are twenty-five areas covering only 1.4 percent of the world's land but home to a whopping forty percent of all known species. Many millions of dollars are going into hotspot conservation. But in 2002 Myers warned, "Most of the hotspots are in developing countries, where they are subject to population pressures among other problems. Within the eight hundred forty thousand square miles of all the hotspots (one-quarter as big again as Alaska), plus their hinterlands totaling another ten percent of Earth's land surface, there are more than 1.2 billion people. That is approximately one-fifth of humankind with an average population density almost twice that of the world and an average annual growth rate almost two-fifths higher than that of the world."[8] It's worse today. Yet Myers stands pretty much alone in warning about overpopulation in hotspots.

Besides growth itself, immigration from poor, high-growth countries to wealthier ones can tear up wilderness homes for endangered wildlife. In a case close to home, unlawful immigrants wound the world-class wilderness of the Mexico-United States border. Here, I'll touch on only one plight from that dryland. The Sonoran pronghorn (wrongly called "antelope") is one of the most endangered beings in the world. It lives in the Sonora-Arizona borderlands and finds its best refuge in the Cabeza Prieta National Wildlife Refuge and Wilderness Area. Or did. According to the *Tucson Citizen* newspaper, much of the unlawful immigration through the Arizona desert "funnels" through a narrow valley in the refuge where the pronghorn have their best habitat. Sometimes two hundred unlawful crossers a night stride through, trampling the rare wildflowers and the plants pronghorn eat and draining or fouling the even rarer waterholes the pronghorn must have. It has long been an open question whether the Sonoran subspecies of pronghorn can be saved, but the horde of immigrants tearing through the pronghorn's wilderness home may be the last straw.[9]

44

Wound 3: Fragmentation of Wildlife Neighborhoods

Whether it is starter-castle "estates" strung along wide freeways farther away from cities and workplaces in the United States or new slash-and-burn crop patches (*milpas*) and logging roads in third-world countries, we throw up barriers and fracture zones that box wild animals into smaller and smaller lots. This cleaves migration north (south below the equator) or to higher elevations as home ranges shift because of climate breakdown. Population growth spreads us into once empty (of Man) lands where wild animals had been free to roam widely before our takeover. The shape or siting of the new settlement web is often more deadly than how many acres are cleared. A few settlers or "estates" with a handful of roads can stomp down a footprint that breaks up a big wildland.

Nonetheless, the sprawl first comes from more men, women, and children. More off-road vehicles tearing up wildlife pathways between summer and winter range come from more people. More people here and there means more blacktop roads in between with curves straightened out for faster driving and thereby more deadly for the lynx or elk that are used to wandering over a once-slow dirt road.

One way to tell what kinds of animals are about is to look at roadkill. The hopeful spread of wolves, lynx, and cougars in the United States is shown but also stopped by deaths along interstate highways and other main roads. More Coloradans, for example, means more cars and pickups and SUVs, which means more upgraded roads, which means more death traps for wildlife.

Wound 4: Upsetting and Weakening Ecological and Evolutionary Processes

Our crowding on the land and further spreading into lands once empty of Man affects ecological and evolutionary processes such as wildfire, river flooding and drying, predation, and pollination. More and more of us squeeze into lush, rank river bottoms and thereby make a "need" for upstream flood-control dams, which then stop healthy hydrological processes. More of us need more water for irrigating crops and making more electricity, both of which call for colossal dams on rivers. In the United States and Canada, the spread of homes into forests leads to putting down natural wildfires. Stopping such lightning-sparked fires harms forest health and sets up the woods for bigger, unhealthy, unquenchable blazes later.

Man, whether Denver suburbanites or Kenyan herders, are unfriendly to big cats, wolves or wild dogs, and other wild hunters. And so as they spread afield, they kill these wild things and the ecosystem loses top-down regulation of prey species.[10] Likewise, people in new settlements of whatever kind don't want beavers or elephants upsetting their high-dollar landscaping or their slash-and-burn cornfields.

When we take over wildlands, we often also make the land unfriendly to native pollinators. Biologists who study pollination, whether by native kinds of bees or moths, hummingbirds, or bats, have warned that many such pollinators are fewer and fewer every year.

Wound 5: Spread of Exotic Species and Diseases

More people everywhere means more ships hauling more species back and forth, which means the spread of non-native species. Pumped-up trade between growing (in population and wealth) countries also spreads invasive species. Freighters bring hitch-hiking harmful exotics, such as zebra and quagga mussels, green crabs, and the spiny water-flea.

When folks go into new lands, they hack out welcome ground for invasive, exotic, weedy life that pushes out native species. Plant diseases, such as Dutch elm disease and chestnut blight, are among the most deadly things spread by trade and shifting settlements. Such ills lead to upheavals in native-plant communities.

Wound 6: Biocide Poisoning of Land, Air, Water, and Wildlife

Back in 1971, biologist Daniel McKinley warned, "All animals create waste, but only man makes products that nature cannot reclaim, and at such a rate that he can spoil the world before it purifies itself."[11] This Man-waste not only sickens and kills children, women, and men, but also even more so harms and kills other Earthlings. People spray and spill biocides and befoul Earth with all kinds of banes. Worldwide, it may seem that people in wealthy lands pollute more than do those of the third-world countries. But down on the ground or in the water, peasants can spread and spill more banes than do most Europeans or Americans. Likewise, Americans in the hinterlands are more lackadaisical in handling them than even suburban yard lords. All too often, the lower on the ladder of income and schooling one goes, whether in Essex County, New York, or the slums of Lagos, the lower the understanding of how awful some chemical brews can be. Thickening settlements lead to even more smoke and filth, many kinds of which are biocides to wild things. The spread of *Homo sapiens*, whether as suburbanites, city dwellers, or peasants onto new lands, brings spilling of pesticides, motor oil, antifreeze, and other nasty crud.

Leaping industrialization in China, India, and other booming third-world countries is happening more sloppily than in other lands. Poisoned, polluted, and dirty land, air, and water exist where there is little or no oversight. The evil banes aren't all homemade, though; some are rich nations' exports of junked computers and other electronic gadgets for recycling—a witch's brew of world and local pollution. In wealthy lands, laws, regulations, and enforcement are better and watchdogging is better. In the third-world countries, there is little oversight of how people deal with toxics, pesticides, and oil.

Wherever pollution exists, growing numbers of us means more spreading of it. Much as we would like to get rid of these problems, we must acknowledge that more of us brings more pollutants and poisons. It's hard to clean up a mess when the number of those making the mess grows every year, sometimes twice as many every score of years.

Wound 7: Climate Change and Ocean Acidification

As early as 1969 Paul Ehrlich and John Holdren saw one of the upshots of overpopulation as a rise in "the atmospheric percentage of CO_2," leading to a "greenhouse effect" (though they didn't use those words yet).[12] Unlike other species, Man lives worldwide. The whole Earth is our home—and our dump. The needed resource that has run out first is not food, water, oil, or rare minerals, but the wherewithal of the atmosphere, seas, and woods to soak up our industrial, transportation, and agricultural belches of carbon dioxide, methane, and other greenhouse gases. The wealthy pump out more greenhouse gases per capita, but third-worlders add much by setting fires in forests, grasslands, and shrublands.

With climate change, a key formula is at work. In 1974, physicist John Holdren and biologist Paul Ehrlich, then both at Stanford University, set down in *Science* the scientific formula *I=PAT*.[13] Paul and Anne Ehrlich spelled out what it means: "The impact of any human group on the environment can be usefully viewed as the product of three different factors. The first is the number of people. The second is some measure of the average person's consumption of resources...Finally, the product of those two factors...is multiplied by an index of the environmental disruptiveness of the technologies that provide the goods consumed...In short, (I) Impact = (P) Population x (A) Affluence (resource consumption) x (T) Technology, or I=PAT."[14] While many see Impact more as harm to the life support system Earth gives Man, I see Impact as the ecological wounds.

When it comes to Wound 7, Affluence (A) and Technology (T) are big players in how much Impact (I) one may have. However, enough small players can outweigh a few big players. What drives the logging and burning of the Amazon rainforest to make new cattle paddocks and soybean fields? Too many people having children in Brazil, plus the swelling numbers of hungry mouths in the rest of the world who crave the food many believe the "last agricultural frontier" can grow. This is leading to more of a jump in Brazil's greenhouse gas load and to the loss of tropical forests that if kept, would go on taking carbon from the atmosphere—and be the dearest pool of manifold life left on Earth.

China has now shot past the United States as the worst greenhouse gas emitter in the world, thanks to its whopping population racing after greater wealth. But if China had only half a billion mouths instead of nearly a billion and a half, it would not have done so. If China's growth had not been slowed by the much-cursed one-child policy, it would be blowing out much more greenhouse pollution than it already is. Without the one-child rule, the Chinese themselves have acknowledged that there would be about four hundred million more Chinese today. However, this did not stop them from easing one-child policies beginning in 2014.

Family planning experts, weighing the threat of greenhouse gas pollution, write in *The Lancet*, "In a world of twelve billion inhabitants, much more severe measures would be needed to stabilise the planet's environment than in a world of eight billion people. Prevention of unwanted births today by family planning might be one of the most cost-effective ways to preserve the planet's environment for the future."[15]

In 2006, then-British Prime Minister Tony Blair acknowledged that it was "now plain that the emission of greenhouse gases, associated with industrialization and economic growth from a world population that has increased six-fold in two hundred years, is causing global warming at a rate that is unsustainable." Alas, Blair is one of the few leaders to acknowledge how the population explosion is behind global warming. The United Kingdom's Optimum Population Trust says, "Policies to tackle climate change, by contrast, almost universally ignore population: it is seen as too sensitive and controversial." The upshot is that the solutions for greenhouse gas pollution are all technical and economic.[16] What is all too often overlooked when it comes to greenhouse gas pollution and all of the *Seven Ecological Wounds*, for that matter? Population growth and overpopulation are the main drivers of these problems, and lowering the population is the main solution.

In a 2007 study, the Optimum Population Trust (OPT) found that forgoing children was the best way to reduce the UK's greenhouse gas load. "Each new UK citizen less means a lifetime carbon dioxide saving of nearly seven hundred fifty tonnes, a climate impact equivalent to six hundred twenty return flights between London and New York." The press release from the Trust goes on to say, "Based on a 'social cost' of carbon dioxide of $85 a tonne, the report estimates the climate cost of each new Briton over their lifetime at roughly £30,000 ($63,240). The lifetime emission costs of the extra ten million people projected for the UK by 2074 would therefore be over £300 billion." "A thirty-five-pence condom, which could avert that £30,000 cost from a single use, thus represents a 'spectacular' potential return on investment—around nine million percent."

The Trust cuts through the fog of climate change with, "The most effective personal climate change strategy is limiting the number of children one has. The most effective national and global climate change strategy is limiting the size of the population." It also sums up the strategy this way, "Population limitation should therefore be seen as the most cost-effective carbon offsetting strategy available to individuals and nations—a strategy that applies with even more force to developed nations such as the UK because of the higher consumption levels."

The Trust makes a sharp warning that must be heeded by all working to cut back on greenhouse gas emissions. "Even if by 2050 the world had managed to achieve a sixty percent cut in its 1990 emission levels, in line with the Intergovernmental Panel on Climate Change's recommendations and UK government's target, almost all of it would be cancelled out by population growth."[17] In a companion briefing, OPT writes, "Put another way, even if the world managed to achieve a fifty-two percent cut in its 1990 emission levels (21.4 billion tonnes) by 2050—not far off the IPCC's sixty percent target—it would be cancelled out by population growth."[18] Why? Over the years the added folks from overbreeding will drive emissions back up.

So, as dreadfully hard as it will be to cut our greenhouse gas emissions, it will be pissin' in the wind without reducing population. Like it or hate it, this is reality. And what the Trust says for greenhouse gas pollution holds true for the other wounds as well.

It is widely known that carbon dioxide is the leading greenhouse pollutant (though pound for pound methane is more harmful). It has been much less widely known that black carbon, or soot, is next. Soot was not even named as "a warming agent in the 2007 summary report by the Intergovernmental Panel on Climate Change."[19] Most of the black carbon now comes from cooking fires of twigs and dried dung in crummy little stoves in the third-world countries. Sadly, it's the only way now that the crammed-together and yet fast-growing crowds of peasants in India and elsewhere have to cook their meals. The crude technology has much to do with this woe, but it is greatly made worse by the swarm of such stoves and by how many more of these poorest of the poor come into the world every year. *The New York Times* reports, "While carbon dioxide may be the No. 1 contributor to rising global temperatures, scientists say, black carbon has emerged as an important No. 2, with recent studies estimating that it is responsible for eighteen percent of the planet's warming, compared with forty percent for carbon dioxide."[20] Soot owns an even greater share of the blame for melting glaciers in the Himalayas and other high mountains, and "might account for as much as half of Arctic warming."[21] When it settles out of the atmosphere, soot makes ice and snow dark, reflecting less of the sun's energy back into space and causing faster melting.

Work is being done to get low-soot cook stoves to folks in need, though getting tradition-bound women to change and cook on them will not be a snap. The write-up in the *Times* rightly nudges the quick spread of better stoves, but nowhere is a word about the most-needed action for third-world soot, which is to freeze and reduce population growth.[22]

I'm not trying to let the U.S. off the hook here. What we've done or haven't done on greenhouse gas pollution has been worse than shameful. Overall, each one of us in the U.S. burps more CO_2 and other greenhouse gases than do folks in any other country in the world, and we are each burping more every day. In the years 1990 to 2003 our "*per capita* CO_2 emissions increased 3.2 percent," write Philip Cafaro and Winthrop Staples. That doesn't tell the whole tale, though. Over that same time, overall U.S. emissions went up much more—by 20.2 percent! How so? Well, our population rose 16.1 percent.[23] In other words, the growing Man swarm of the United States was about five times more to blame for our greater greenhouse pollution than was the rise from each of us.

As we mull over what leads to each of these seven wounds in the U.S. and worldwide, we must acknowledge that Affluence and Technology play a large part. Nonetheless, we cannot let that overshadow the way overpopulation and high growth drive ecological wounds, whether straightforward killing of threatened Earthlings or cranking out carbon dioxide, methane, and other heat-trapping gases.

World Upshot

For much of Asia, Latin America, and Africa since the end of World War II, there has been a mind-numbing onslaught against wilderness and wildlife. It has also been a time of head-spinning population growth in the same lands. This is not happenstance. Population growth has been the main axe hacking at the tree of life.

The following table shows population growth in some countries of outstanding worth in wildlife; these are also the countries that have had the population bomb go off and that have gobbled up much of their wild web. When you look at this table, you will see how much the Man swarm has grown since World War II, and how much the United Nations and others forecast that the Man swarm will keep growing until 2050.

This quick look at one hundred years has much to teach. In no way do I wish to downplay the might of globalization and the way the United States, China, Japan, Europe, and a few others ransack the rest of the world for raw goods. However, leapfrogging growth in even the most technologically backward lands also puts an unbearable squeeze on wild things and wildlands. The kind of growth we see in this table is like the growth of a metastasizing cancer.

You'll also see that for each of these countries, I've listed a few of the wild ones threatened by growth. Overall, the point of this table is to plainly see that countries with some of the most highly endangered species in the world are still undergoing a massive population explosion, and population forecasts for 2050 in these countries paint a most dire picture for the future of wild things. It shows the reality that the more population grows, the more Man eats Earth, and the deeper the ecological wounds go.[24]

POPULATION GROWTH IN COUNTRIES OF HIGH BIODIVERSITY

COUNTRY	POP 1940-50	POP 2010	POP 2050	2010 % <15	Threatened and Endangered Species
Afghanistan	12 m	29.1 m	53.4 m	42.9%	Snow Leopard
Belize	65,000	314,522	543,690	37.3%	Jaguar, Coral Reefs, Tapir
Bolivia	3.8 m	9.9 m	16 m	35.1%	Spectacled Bear, Vicuna
Botswana	285,000	2 m	2.9 m	34.3%	Lion, Elephant, Wild Dog
Brazil	47.2 m	201.1 m	260.7 m	26.5%	Jaguar, Maned Wolf, Giant Otter
China	430 m	1,330 m	1,304 m	17.9%	Panda, Amur Leopard, Hainan Gibbon, Tiger
Congo (Zaire)	10.7 m	70.9 m	189.3 m	46.7%	Mt. and Lowland Gorillas, Bonobo, Okapi
Costa Rica	772,000	4.5 m	6.1 m	25%	Jaguar, Quetzal
Ethiopia	6.8 m	88 m	278.3 m	46.2%	Ethiopian Wolf, Grevy's Zebra
Honduras	1.2 m	8 m	12.9 m	37.4%	Jaguar, Tigrillo
India	314 m	1,173.1 m	1,656.6 m	30.1%	Tiger, Rhino, Elephant, Lion, Lion-tailed Macaque
Indonesia	72 m	243 m	313 m	27.7%	Tiger, Elephant, Rhino, Bay Cat
Iran	13.9 m	76.9 m	100 m	21.3%	Cheetah, Sturgeon
Iraq	4.1 m	29.7 m	56.3 m	38.4%	Leopard, Wolf
Kenya	4.2 m	40 m	65.2 m	42.3%	Lion, White & Black Rhinos, Wild Dog
Liberia	1.6 m	3.7 m	8.2 m	44.3%	Pygmy Hippo, Chimpanzee
Madagascar	4.4 m	21.3 m	56.5 m	43.3%	Lemur species, Fossa
Mexico	19.6 m	112.5 m	147.9 m	28.7%	Jaguar, Scarlet Macaw, Thick-bill Parrot, Vaquita

POPULATION GROWTH IN COUNTRIES OF HIGH BIODIVERSITY (CONTINUED)

Mozambique	5.5 m	22.1 m	41.8 m	44.1%	Elephant, Lion
Myanmar (Burma)	16.9 m	53.4 m	70.7 m	27.9%	Tiger, Lesser Muntjac, Malayan Tapir
Nepal	6.5 m	29 m	46 m	35.6%	Tiger, Rhino, Snow Leopard, Musk Deer
Nigeria	23 m	152.2 m	264.3 m	41.2%	Gorilla, Chimpanzee
Peru	7.9 m	29.9 m	38.6 m	28.5%	Andean Mt. Cat, Huemul, Spectacled Bear
Philippines	18.5 m	99.9 m	172 m	34.9%	Monkey-eating Eagle, Tamarau
Sudan	7.5 m	43.9 m	97.2 m	40.2%	Elephant, Lion, Addax
Thailand	20 m	67.1 m	71.1 m	20.3%	Tiger, Elephant, Fea's Muntjac
Turkey	20 m	77.8 m	101 m	26.9%	Leopard, Brown Bear
Uganda	3.9 m	33.4 m	128 m	50%	Chimpanzee, Mt. Gorilla
Venezuela	4.3 m	27.2 m	40.3 m	30%	Jaguar, Harpy Eagle
Vietnam*	25.5 m	89.6 m	111.2 m	25.6%	Tiger, Saola
Laos		6.4 m	10.1 m	40.5%	Tiger, Giant Muntjac
Cambodia		14.5 m	22.3 m	32.2%	Tiger, Clouded Leopard
TOTAL	25.5 m	110.5 m	143.6 m		
Zambia	1.7 m	13.5 m	38.4 m	44.8%	Lion, Elephant, Rhino
Zimbabwe	1.8 m	11.7 m	25.2 m	43.1%	Elephant, W & B Rhino

* Before 1950, Vietnam, Laos, and Cambodia were French Indochina.

5

THE CORNUCOPIAN MINDSET

We now have in our hands—in our libraries, really—the technology to feed, clothe, and supply energy to an ever-growing population for the next seven billion years.[1]
—*Julian Simon*

The late Julian Simon, professor of business administration at the University of Maryland, was the darling of free marketers who truly believe that even the sky is not the limit. But it's not just free marketers who think this. Barry Commoner, a socialist and early pollution fighter, said, "It is a spurious ideal to claim that rising population anywhere in the world is responsible for the deteriorating environment."[2] Simon and Commoner show how those with diverging social and political positions can have the same mindset that growth is nothing to worry about.

I call this mindset "cornucopian." The cornucopia, from Greek mythology, is a goat's horn overflowing with fruit, vegetables, and grain that is always refilled with whatever one wishes. It stands for everlasting fullness and wealth. Today, those who pooh-pooh worries about limits to growth and overpopulation are modern day cornucopians.

Cutting Across Political Lines

Ideologically speaking, cornucopians shut out any thought of limits. Even some who back many conservation and environmental steps cannot bring themselves to believe that Earth and its "resources" are not endless. Let me keep on my path with Simon and Commoner and take the two political bookends—Marxists and free-market boosters—to show how today's society believes in ever-growing wealth. Those in between—the whole political bookshelf—also share such cornucopian dreams. This widespread belief in endless progress is why the worldwide establishment will not work to stop growth, why it cannot fathom the end of growth, and why ongoing growth is a "given."

In the shallow, unecological way many of us seem to look at everything, economic libertarianism and Marxism seem far away from each other. If we look deeper, however, we find that Marxism and libertarianism share an underlying view of humans foremost as economic beings. They both see Earth as an overflowing warehouse for industrial civilization, a warehouse that is never empty.[3] Unclouded British conservationist Sandy Irvine writes that "the right-wing economist Julian Simon has revived [Marx's Labor Theory of value] as the theory of People as the Ultimate Resource."[4]

Both Marxism and free marketism have swapped God for Man. They see eye-to-eye that:

Man is rational.
Man is a blank slate.
Man is an economic being.
Progress is perfecting individual humans.
The world is a warehouse.
Growth is good.
Progress is foretold.
There are no limits, or any limits
can be overcome by technology.

They also share a godless yet supernatural belief of how things work—historical determinism. Each thinks its economic-political-social order is not just the best, but is somehow foreordained by history as its end. True believers of both cults see the workers' state or the free market as some abstract ideal or Platonic essence that has been waiting in the wings for the right time to be birthed into being by history. The key to either being seen as the "end of history" is that the resources on which each is grounded are endless.

In 1977, during the Cold War, cultural anthropologist Marvin Harris wrote, "Thanks to science and engineering, the average standard of living in the industrial nations is higher than at any time in the past. This fact, more than any other, bolsters our faith that progress is inevitable—a faith, incidentally, shared as much by the Comintern [Communist International] as by the U.S. Chamber of Commerce."[5]

In *The Arrogance of Humanism*, Rutgers biologist David Ehrenfeld warns that this faith, which he calls humanism, sits on a stack of assumptions, which "cut across political lines":

All problems are soluble by people.
Many problems are soluble by technology.
Those problems that are not soluble by technology, or
by technology alone, have solutions in the social world
(of politics, economics, etc.).
When the chips are down, we will apply ourselves and
work together for a solution before it is too late.
Some resources are infinite; all finite or limited resources
have substitutes.
Human civilization will survive.[6]

This kind of faith scraps even the *thought* of limits.

The Idea of Progress

Anthropocentric arrogance is wrapped up with "The Idea of Progress," a rather new whimsy in Western Civilization holding that civilization is a steady march of betterment with no end in sight. As we read cornucopian forecasts, we can see how The Idea of Progress bucks up the faith. And The Idea of Progress has a breathtakingly wide sweep, which is why even many conservation and environmental leaders cling to it. Keep in mind, though, that the founders of the wilderness movement—Aldo Leopold, Benton MacKaye, Robert Sterling Yard, Bob Marshall, and others—were strongly driven by antimodernist fears. Read Paul Sutter's *Driven Wild* to learn how early wilderness conservationists stood against go-go-boosterism. They did not believe that we could have both wilderness and a bandwagon of gadgets, or that we could have both wildlife and never-slowing growth.[7] Today we need to go back to the wisdom of these elders.

While today's environmentalist and conservation leaders are mostly in the grip of a progress mindset, some thinkers outside the environmental movement are more willing to look at the pitfalls of population growth. Former *Wall Street Journal* reporter Robert Merry weighs The Idea of Progress in his thought-sparking, forthright book, *Sands of Empire.* He warns, "It's one thing to talk about man's seemingly inexorable advances in scientific knowledge…It is something else entirely to suggest…that these advances actually are altering and improving the nature of man…"[8] Longtime science journalist Eugene Linden writes, "Any vision of the future that either expects or demands a new human, a higher consciousness, or some other transformation of human nature should be automatically suspect."[9] The Idea of Progress, whatever the political or ethnic getup it wears (and it wears many), loudly calls for such a vision.

When English settlers from crowded, picked-over Europe clambered ashore in the New World in the 1600s they found what seemed to them an endless wealth of game, fish, furs, timber, firewood, fat land, and elbowroom. They waxed about such superabundance and believed that it could never end.[10] We are truly their children.

Today's wrangles about dwindling ocean fish stocks, stripping of forests, suburban sprawl, climate change, and so on are a death match between the myth of superabundance and new scientific understandings of ecological carrying capacity on a finite Earth. It is hard to let go of the cuddling belief in superabundance and think about population limits when one is not schooled in science—as many economists and environmentalists are not.

Cornucopian Myth

Two generations ago, the American and world Establishment was caught up in "the golden optimism of the 1950s." One report from the Rockefeller Panel foresaw, "New technologies, more efficient extraction processes, [and] new uses may open up new worlds. Even now we can discern the outlines of a future in which, through the use of the split atom, our resources of both power and raw materials will be limitless..."[11] In 1951, *Time* magazine fawned over Bureau of Reclamation engineers. One article with the bullish title, "Endless Frontier," gushed that "irrigation experts are now convinced that the rapidly growing U.S. can expand almost indefinitely within its boundaries."[12] In 1966, *Time* whooped that everyone in the U.S. would be independently wealthy by 2000 and that only ten percent of the population would have to work. The magazine quoted RAND Corporation scientists who blissed how "huge fields of kelp and other kinds of seaweed will be tended by undersea 'farmers'—frogmen who will live for months at a time in submerged bunkhouses...This will provide at least a 'partial answer' to doomsdayers who worry about the prospects of starvation for a burgeoning world population."[13]

However, the cornucopians did not have the floor to themselves. It was a rough and tumble time. In 1960, Edward Deevey, Jr. took a sweeping look at population in *Scientific American*. As for those with wild-eyed dreams of much, much bigger human populations on Earth, he wrote: "If my new figures are correct, the population could theoretically increase by thirty to forty times. But man would have to displace all other herbivores and utilize all the vegetation with the ten percent efficiency established by the ecological rule of tithes. No land that now supports greenery could be spared for nonagricultural purposes; the populace would have to reside in the polar regions, or on artificial 'green islands in the sea'...scummed over, of course, by ten inches of Chlorella Culture."[14]

In 1967, *Time* magazine made the "25 and Under" generation "Man of the Year" and brayed, "He is the man who will land on the moon, cure cancer and the common cold, lay out blight-proof, smog-free cities, enrich the underdeveloped world and, no doubt, write finis to poverty and war."[15] Well, "he" did land on the moon. To be fair, some folks got some things right. I have to give a nod to uber-optimists Herman Kahn and Anthony Wiener in 1967 for one of the "One hundred technical innovations very likely in the last third of the twentieth century"—"31. Some control of weather and/or climate."[16]

In 1974, Nobel Laureate in Economics Robert Solow wrote, "It is very easy to substitute other factors for natural resources, then...The world can, in effect, get along without natural resources, so exhaustion is just an event, not a catastrophe."[17] I wonder if he would have changed his mind if he had to step out of the abstract and into the real? Would he have thought facing dying of hunger or thirst was an event, not a catastrophe?

Solow's world that could get along without natural resources was a world only of humans. Utterly unknown to him was the world of other Earthlings, in which, as Philip Cafaro of Colorado State University wrote me, "Other species cannot substitute one resource for another: lose snail populations, and lose the Everglades kite; lose large cavity-nesting trees, and ivory-billed woodpeckers go extinct. Concern for other species is not a requirement for winning the Nobel Prize in Economics."

The cornucopian mood was well put by economist George Gilder in 1981 when he wrote, "The United States must overcome the materialistic fallacy: the illusion that resources and capital are essentially things which can run out..." A more rational economist, Allen Kneese, recognized in 1988 that Gilder's kind of economics was "a perpetual motion machine."[18] Kneese wasn't the first to see this. After the 1972 United Nations Conference on the Human Environment in Stockholm, Paul Ehrlich wrote about the back-and-forth between economists and scientists there on sustainability, "As each new perpetual-motion-machine was propounded, one of the biologists or physicists would simply point out that it violated the second law. Finally, in frustration, one of the economists blurted out, 'Who knows what the second law of thermodynamics will be like in a hundred years?'"[19]

It's bad enough that neoclassical economists do not believe in biology, but they do not even believe in physics! Or, as Kenneth Boulding, once president of the American Economic Association, said, "Only madmen and economists believe in perpetual exponential growth."[20] I daresay that some investors and homeowners who believed in perpetual exponential growth in 2008 have rethought their beliefs.

Some cornucopians, however, do believe in resources and even that they can be exhausted. But so what? In 1986, the U.S. National Research Council wrote in a panel report, "Unless one is more concerned with the welfare of people born in the distant future than those born in the immediate future, there is little reason to be concerned about the rate at which population growth is depleting the stock of exhaustible resources."[21] This is like saying, "Long live shortsightedness! Who cares about the grandkids!"

One of today's cornucopians who gushes with happy news is Gregg Easterbrook. He is thought of as one of America's "public intellectuals," and in 2006, he had a piece in the *Los Angeles Times* to celebrate the coming of the three hundred millionth American. This shows how matchless he is as a lover of population growth: "But the rising population also is a fantastic achievement. It means ever-more people are alive to experience love, hope, freedom and the daily miracle of the rising sun. None of us who today enjoy the privilege of being Americans should want to deny this privilege to the many more to come."[22] Now that is cornucopianism.

Arithmetic and Julian Simon

Julian Simon saying, "We now have in our hands—in our libraries, really—the technology to feed, clothe, and supply energy to an ever-growing population for the next seven billion years," is the most straightforward utterance of irrational exuberance among cornucopians.[23] Let's talk a little arithmetic. Seven *billion* years, he said. The planet Earth came into being only about four-and-a-half billion years ago. Life first wriggled no more than four billion years ago. Most animal phyla evolved less than six hundred million years ago, and hominins split off from chimpanzees about five million years ago. Farming and settled life did not sprout until ten thousand years ago. The first civilization started less than seven thousand years ago. Yet, Simon believed that human population could keep growing for seven billion years. Think about that: It is *one million times the length of time human civilization has lasted so far.*

In 1994, the year in which Simon crowed about seven billion years, world population was doubling every forty-three years. At this speed in only 774 years there would be "ten human beings for each square meter of ice-free land on the planet," write Paul and Anne Ehrlich. To get a feeling for this, get four yardsticks and nine friends. Make a square with the yardsticks. Then stand inside with your friends.

In *Betrayal of Science and Reason* Paul and Anne Ehrlich write, "After 1900 years at this growth rate, the mass of the human population would be equal to the mass of the Earth; after 6000 years, the mass of the human population would equal the mass of the universe."[24] Now, I know the Ehrlichs and they are kind and fair. So, they cut Professor Simon a great deal of slack and used a growth rate "*one million times* smaller than the actual 1994 value—that is, if it were only an infinitesimal 0.0000016 percent per year—Earth's population would still reach a mass exceeding that of the universe before the end of the seven-billion-year period Simon mentioned."[25] Simon's belief, then, is witless. Even feckless.

The late University of Colorado physics professor emeritus Al Bartlett wrote that some of his friends quizzed Julian Simon after his seven-billion-year statement and Simon backtracked that he meant only seven *million* years. A billion years is one thousand million years, so Simon was off a bit. Bartlett whipped out his calculator and calculated what would happen if we grew only one percent for seven million years. He got 2.3×10^{30410}. He said, "This is a fairly large number!" The number of atoms in the universe is only about 3×10^{85}. The first number is thirty kilo-orders of magnitude bigger than the number of atoms in the universe. So, if Simon only wanted the number of people to equal the number of atoms in the universe, how long would it take to get there at a growth rate of one percent? All of seventeen thousand years.[26]

If you heard a disheveled street-corner prophet spouting that we could keep growing for seven billion (or million) years, you would chuckle and keep on walking. However, Julian Simon was not a homeless schizophrenic. He was (and still is) the most gushed-over no-limits-to-growth economist for the *Wall Street Journal* crowd. The sheer silliness of Simon's seven-billion (or million, who cares?) big talk shows that the cornucopians are dwelling in a dream world inside their heads and not in the world of earth, fire, air, and water. Long before technology brought us the world of gaming, cornucopians had made up their own. It is way beyond time to start showing people just how far from Earth Simon believers are.

Now, I am no whiz at arithmetic. However, even I can understand Al Bartlett when he teaches simple math to the cornucopians. Bartlett wrote that a round Earth is a problem because a "sphere is bounded and hence is finite." He sees "a new paradigm…emerging which seems to be a return to the wisdom of the ancients." "The pro-growth people say that perpetual growth on this earth is possible. If the pro-growth people are correct, what kind of earth are we living on?"

Bartlett answered that: "[A] flat earth can accommodate growth forever, because a flat earth can be infinite in the two horizontal dimensions and also in the vertical downward direction. The infinite horizontal dimensions forever remove any fear of crowding as population grows, and the infinite downward dimension assures humans of an unlimited supply of all of the mineral raw materials that will be needed by a human population that continues to grow forever."[27]

So, the cornucopians are flat-Earthers. What does that tell you?

Beyond Just Spreading the Wealth

When it comes to sustainability, a lot of people believe all we have to do is be better at spreading the wealth. Sandy Irvine brings them down to Earth in "The Great Denial." He writes, "Studies in Guatemala, for example, show that the benefits of land redistribution would disappear within a generation simply because of population growth."[28] This is not a brush-off of the fairness and need for land redistribution, just an acknowledgment that poverty alleviation and social justice reforms are hopeless without population stabilization and reduction.

In 1994, Hardin showed the blunder of the social justice foes of population planning: "Promoters of 'ethnic power' love to scold rich countries for urging a lower birth rate in poor countries; the ethnics call this 'genocide.' But if a country is poor and powerless because it already has too many children for its resources, it will become even poorer and more powerless if it breeds more. If ethnic pronatalists have their way, poor countries will be ruined."[29]

And what Hardin foresaw in 1994—too many children—has wrecked poor countries. Think of Niger, Rwanda, Mali, Ethiopia, Sudan, Bangladesh, Yemen, Somalia, Honduras…All lands with too many babies.

Maybe the thought of scarcity itself is what's wrong. Hardin wrote, "The idea of scarcity also needs examining, if we are not to be bewitched by words. The problem of poverty is almost invariably seen as one of *shortages*—shortages of supply. But note: poverty can just as logically be seen as a problem of *longages*—longages of demand."[30] Said another way, a shortage occurs when there is excess demand; in the case of food and people, a shortage of food can just as well be seen as a longage of people—aka: overpopulation.

Those who believe the cornucopian myth need to be reminded of Man's history and prehistory. Archaeologist Steven LeBlanc writes that "there is no evidence—not in the archaeological, ethnographic, or historical records—that humans have ever attained [ecological] balance for more than a couple of centuries anywhere on Earth. All humans grow, impact their environment, and, sooner or later, exceed the carrying capacity."[31]

We need to take this history to heart, see past cornucopian myths, and keep our feet grounded in the real world—one with true realities of exponential growth and resulting overpopulation.

6

BIRTH DEARTH FOLLIES

We geezers can still work.

—Susan Morgan

In 2004, demographer Phillip Longman wrote in the journal *Foreign Affairs,* "Most people think overpopulation is one of the worst dangers facing the globe. In fact, the opposite is true. As countries get richer, their populations age and their birthrates plummet. And this is not just a problem of rich countries; the developing world is also getting older fast. Falling birthrates might seem beneficial, but the *economic* and *social* price is too steep to pay. The right policies could help turn the tide, but only if enacted before it's too late."[1] (my italics) Folks like Longman, who see decreases in population as cause for concern, can be called "birth dearthers."

Japan and a few European countries have not only slowed how fast their populations are rising but also have brought them down to replacement or even to where their many footprints will slowly ebb. They have gained what many conservationists, environmentalists, and others have long worked for. But, instead of marking this wonderful fulfillment with thousands of popping champagne corks raining down as condoms, the birth dearthers are warning of doom.

Joining Longman are shortsighted analysts and government leaders who are overwrought with what they see as the economic and social woes of fewer births. From Italy and Greece to South Korea and Japan, governments have offered cash and other benefits to women for having more than two children. What are Longman and the others in a cold sweat about? There may be fewer working-age people to underwrite pension plans for retirees. Schools overbuilt from the Baby Boom may shutter. Hinterland villages might become emptier. And big-breeding clans might overrun smaller-breeding clans. Are these nightmares the whole of it? I'm afraid so. That's all there is. And when we look more sharply, we might even say that there is no there there.

The birth-dearth worry comes from a narrow and shallow mindset. Birth dearthers sweat over a slight shift in age within wealthy societies and how that might make it tougher to underwrite fat retirement policies for oldsters. They want more births so there will be more workers to put up the money for retirees. Or, they want loads of young immigrants to tilt the age ratio. In other words, swell all the ills of overshooting carrying capacity, to ensure more human "capital," more cogs in our country's economic machine.

The first thing to understand about birth-dearth fears is that they are only economic and social. They are *not* ecological. Not even a teeny bit. They are about a world that has no life other than Man. Dealing with the economic and social plights tied to slowing births is child's play compared to the ecological prices of through-the-roof populations and overshooting carrying capacity.

Birth-dearthers don't weigh the ecological outcomes. So we must. We must draw serious attention to the ecological impact of the population explosion. We need to be willing to talk about the following:

❖ Women are choosing to have fewer children for their own life's good and economic well-being. It is a big step backward for governments to once again see women as breeders for more taxpayers.

❖ "Fears" about steady or even slowly ebbing populations are economic, social, and political, not ecological.

❖ The whole birth-dearth idea may be best seen as a clever scam run by those who get rich from growth. I am loath to see conspiracies, but given the cunning of some industries to mislead people, we need to look at this with a sharp eye. Cigarette tobacco, the ozone hole, and greenhouse gases are a few earlier plays of this kind.[2]

❖ Seniors are not the only ones who lean on working-age men and women. Babies and children do, too. When calculating percentages of working-age and nonworking-age people, the birth dearthers leave out children. This shows how shallow their thinking is.

❖ Worries about lopsidedness between retirees and those paying into pensions can be straightforwardly dealt with now by raising the retirement age a few years. As Susan Morgan says, "We geezers can still work." Steve Camarota, Director of Research at the Center for Immigration Studies, takes the same tack. Instead of raising immigration to deal with the "dependence ratio" plight, Camarota says a slight raising of the retirement age would do it.[3] Just a little number crunching shows the phony plight birth dearthers have brewed up.

❖ Population growth must stop. It will be much harder to deal with the economic shift later when there are even more bodies to feed and house, and to care for in old age. Birth dearthers don't seem to have thought this far into tomorrow.

❖ The worst outcomes of population growth are ecological. Climate change, habitat withering, and mass extinction are far harder to work out when there are more people.

❖ If we want to weigh social and economic plights, then feeding, housing, and caring for billions more is far tougher than a retirement woe.

❖ Lastly, we can pitch the overwrought worries of the birth dearthers as being not about a true threat, but rather as a soft puzzle to be worked out by the genius of the free-market system.

The fact is, Man has already overshot ecological carrying capacity on Earth. The Earth's carrying capacity at a European standard of living is at best five billion fewer people than live today—or less than two billion (don't get shaken; two billion was Earth's population in 1927). One of the few bright spots on the skyline is that population growth in many of the wealthiest countries—which are those that do the worst harm to worldwide carrying capacity and the health of wild things—has stopped, and in a few is beginning to slightly ebb. This is wonderful; something to be cheered, not dreaded. What better, happier job could we have than to figure out how a no-growth society should work and what landscapes to rewild? What a top-notch puzzle for the sharp minds of the free-market!

In the end, what plight would come if the species of Man lessened? The birth-dearth fears and calls for more babies are truly much ado about nothing. But they click with something in the mind of Man. Something in there is afraid of a population running flat. If our community doesn't grow, we feel that we have failed. The birth dearth has become a slice of the popular wisdom among public intellectuals who, in their ecologically shallow brains, never think of asking bedrock questions about carrying capacity or about the welfare of other Earthlings.

We who understand carrying capacity and love wild things need to knock down birth-dearth fears whenever we hear them.

WAS PAUL EHRLICH REALLY WRONG?

During the 1980s, some of the worst famines in history afflicted large parts of Africa and South Asia, under the very noses of the United Nations and other international agencies. In absolute numbers, more illiterate, impoverished, and chronically malnourished people live in the world at the end of the twentieth century than at the beginning.[1]

—*Marvin Harris*

One way cornucopians sweep away worry about overpopulation is by targeting how population biologist Paul Ehrlich's warnings about a great starvation in his famous book, *The Population Bomb*, did not come true.[2] Plenty of people think Ehrlich was blowing smoke. Was he? Let me shed some light on the misunderstanding.

Consider the Times in which Ehrlich Wrote

The Population Bomb was written in 1968. It was a book of its time and should be read in that light. At the time, family planning and much of what we take for granted with birth control today was not widespread and was still a hot potato. Abortion was still unlawful in most states.

In 1968, population growth was outstripping food growing, and widespread starvation was seen as something that could happen. This was before the "Green Revolution," which goosed up how much food could be grown worldwide, thanks mostly to fossil fuels and increased irrigation. Better kinds of crops helped, but the significance of this has been overstated. More fertilizers and pesticides were key, and were made mostly from petroleum. Since this time, thousands of irrigation dams have been built all over the world, and the building has been done with fossil fuels. Gasoline-powered well drilling and water pumps have irrigated millions of acres. Tractors and other farm machinery running on gasoline and diesel have become much more widespread since 1968.

When you read *The Population Bomb*, it can be easy to get somewhat taken aback by its apocalyptic feeling. But it needs to be taken in context; it *was* an apocalyptic time. A world war was much worried about then. The Cuban Missile Crisis had happened only a few years earlier. The Vietnam War was going badly, and there was fear of Chinese swarming in from the north. Red China was thought to be a great threat; Nixon had not yet opened the door to diplomatic relations. Fifteen years earlier we had been in a major land war with Red China in Korea.

And in 1968, population growth had not yet slowed down anywhere. It was still raining babies in the United States, Europe, and Japan. Millions were starving in China due to shortfalls in food growing. Understanding what the world was like in 1968 sheds light on the scenarios in *The Population Bomb* about widespread, deadly starvation leading to world war with Red China. At the time, this was seen a realistic fear.

Ehrlich Wrote Scenarios, not Predictions

When it comes to *The Population Bomb*, few books have been more misquoted or misunderstood. Cornucopians say that Ehrlich was making hard predictions, when in fact he was merely throwing onto the table a handful of possible scenarios for the future. His scenarios, and those of other population writers, were for the worst outcomes if we didn't do anything to head them off. Ehrlich and others weren't writing only to scare folks; they were writing to wake up everyone so they would do something to head off the worst.

Shortsightedness

The truth is, some of the worst scenarios in *The Population Bomb* could *yet* happen. *Yet* is the key word.

The worst of the ugly overpopulation scenarios hasn't happened—yet. Nonetheless, millions have died or have been made wretched thanks to population growth since 1968. More starvation may be on the way. When? I don't know. But I do know that right now we are scalping millions of acres of wildlands that are the homes for thousands of kinds of threatened wildlife. I know that right now we are sucking the oceans clean of fish for our snowballing populations to eat. The worst for Man is still up ahead. The worst for all the other Earthlings is right now—and if we don't start reducing population, it will get even worse.

Ehrlich Offered Answers and Many Were Followed

Widely overlooked by those who snort at *The Population Bomb* is that Ehrlich offered a ladder of steps to head off starvation. Among them was all-out work to increase agricultural productivity. With the Green Revolution this was done and crop yields per acre rose. But much of the Green Revolution came from petroleum: fertilizer, pesticides, herbicides, and fuel to run irrigation pumps and tractors. Improved crops helped, but not as much as technological optimists want to believe. All together, improved crops from agricultural scientists such as Norman Borlaug and the heavy use of fossil fuels and artificial fertilizer led to a rise of two percent a year in grain yield per acre all over the world from 1950 to 1990. In the last twenty years though, yield has been going up only one percent a year or has flatlined.

Technological optimists think that genetic reengineering will lead to another Green Revolution. Experts think differently. Take Lester Brown, agricultural analyst and founder of the Worldwatch Institute, who pricks hope-bubbles of technological optimists when he writes, "Unfortunately, however, no genetically modified crops have led to dramatically higher yields…Nor do they seem likely to do so, simply because conventional plant-breeding techniques have already tapped most of the potential for raising crop yields."[3]

Ehrlich and others called to make family planning widespread worldwide. Much of the drive for the strong work to get birth control into the hands of women was thanks to Ehrlich and others waking up world leaders and people around the world. Thanks to Ehrlich, international birth control became a big deal. Not only in Europe and Japan and North America did birth rates come down sharply thanks to this campaign, but so did birth rates in many third-world countries as well. China, perhaps, showed the most gumption of any country in this undertaking (they had the worst threat staring them in the eyes, too) and cut births back amazingly. If you look at the third-world countries that worked hardest at lowering births in the 1960s and 1970s, you will also see that those countries have done much better economically.

Without *The Population Bomb* and other "doom and gloom" warnings, things would be much worse for people today, and we could have already cracked the ten billion mark.

Famine has Happened and is still Happening

Some who dismiss *The Population Bomb* and the writings of other doomsayers make it seem as though everyone is well fed in today's world and that the threat of famines has passed. This isn't so. Starvation has struck time and time again since 1968. Remember Ethiopia? Remember Somalia? How about North Korea? Afghanistan? China?

In truth, between 1968 and 1996, two hundred fifty million people died from starvation. This is about what the population of the United States was in 1996. Nearly ten million children a year have died from "hunger and hunger-related diseases" since *The Population Bomb* was written.[4] More than fifty countries that had fed themselves in the 1930s were net importers of food by the 1980s.[5] That statistic stands as one of the most hard-hitting truths about population growth and food production. Cornucopians utter not a word about these fifty. The hallowed leap in crop yield has happened in only some lands. In these other fifty during the Green Revolution, population grew faster than crop production. Insofar as tomorrow goes, if you want to know why the world will shortly be a hungry world, read Lester Brown's book, *Outgrowing the Earth.*[6] It is full of facts, figures, and disturbing predictions.

After listing a few of the wars and internal fights wracking the world at the end of the twentieth century, distinguished anthropologist Marvin Harris wrote, "As one of these conflicts ends, another begins: Nothing warrants the hope that the rate of carnage is about to slacken."[7] Furthermore, "During the 1980s, some of the worst famines in history afflicted large parts of Africa and South Asia, under the very noses of the United Nations and other international agencies. In absolute numbers, more illiterate, impoverished, and chronically malnourished people live in the world at the end of the twentieth century than at the beginning."[8]

What Harris writes is important for understanding today's lay of the land. Thanks to the hard work, heart-felt caring for others, billions of dollars from wealthy countries, and the Green Revolution, hundreds of millions more are now threatened by starvation than in 1968. This is the sad thing. Doing good for those alive today sometimes sets up tomorrow to be worse than it would have been if nothing had been done.

And the Green Revolution, with its leaning on fossil fuels, helped lead to greater greenhouse gas pollution. So did other technological "fixes" that helped us to further overshoot carrying capacity. Such bad "side effects" will harm hundreds of millions of the world's poorest folks. Whichever way we turn, it seems that humanitarian and managerial successes can only make things better if they are wrapped up in work for population stabilization and reduction.

The Population Bomb was a Roaring Success

The Population Bomb and the warnings that came with it woke people up to the threat of overpopulation. This helped lead to population control efforts and to ways of growing more food.

Would these have happened without the success of *The Population Bomb*? I think not. So those like Paul Ehrlich who warned us about overpopulation in the 1960s and are now pooh-poohed may be the ones most responsible for their frightening scenarios not coming true. Chew on that.

The Great Bet Myth

Those who say population growth is nothing to worry about often bring up a famous bet between Paul Ehrlich and Julian Simon, which Ehrlich "lost." This bet is brought up to refute Ehrlich and those who warn about overpopulation and overshooting carrying capacity.

In truth however, the bet had nothing to do with carrying capacity. It was about whether the price of five metals would go up or down over a set time of ten years. As Paul Sabin writes in *The Bet: Paul Ehrlich, Julian Simon, and Our Gamble over Earth's Future*, "Ehrlich thought rising metal prices would prove that population growth causes resource scarcity." Simon, on the other hand, believing in the endless cleverness of Man, "argued that markets and new technologies would drive prices down," which would prove that "society did not face resource constraints."[9] It really had nothing to do with whether or not Earth could house greater and greater swarms of Man.

Paul and Anne Ehrlich thoroughly debunk the bet myth in their book, *Betrayal of Science and Reason*. The subtitle of this top-notch book, *How Anti-Environmental Rhetoric Threatens Our Future*, tells us what the book is about. In it Paul and Anne go through antiscientific myths and lies and slay each one of them.

What happened to the metal prices? Prices of three of the metals went down somewhat and two went up, so, since the bet was $200 for each, Simon owed $400 and Ehrlich owed $600. Ehrlich and his fellows lost $200 in all. That was all there was to the bet.

A few years later, Julian Simon wrote in the *San Francisco Chronicle*, "Every measure of material and environmental welfare in the United States and in the world has improved rather than deteriorated. All long-run trends point in exactly the opposite direction from the projections of the doomsayers."[10] Simon was so sure of himself that he offered to bet on his belief. Paul Ehrlich and climatologist Stephen Schneider took Simon on and made fifteen predictions of things getting worse, from per capita cropland decline to buildup of greenhouse gases to per capita firewood decline to extinction to AIDS deaths.[11] All fifteen are listed and explained in *Betrayal of Science and Reason*.[12]

What was Simon's response to betting on these predictions? He wouldn't take the bet. So I say whenever you hear someone bring up the metal-price bet and that Simon won that bet, bring up the later bet to put the historic "bet" between the two men in its place.

The truth is, Ehrlich was *not* wrong. His book, *The Population Bomb*, is far more on target than not. In no way can one say that Ehrlich and others with his thinking have been disproved. It is an outlandish myth. Don't believe it. And please shoot it down when you hear it.

However, the weakness of *The Population Bomb* and most other overpopulation warnings is that they don't deal with how population growth and overpopulation wrecks the wild world.

And that is the really big deal.

8

A HISTORY OF THINKING
ABOUT MAN'S LIMITS

Growth for the sake of growth is
the ideology of the cancer cell.

—*Edward Abbey*

We know the outcomes of overshooting carrying capacity:
(1) hunger and starvation because we can't grow enough
food; (2) squandering natural resources (raw goods) until we run
out; (3) landscalping and the loss of land fertility; (4) cultural,
economic, and political upheaval; and (5) wounds to wild things.
In this chapter, let's take a look at the twenty-five hundred year
history of warnings and worries about this overshoot. As you will
see, population growth and warnings about overpopulation lurk
in this history.

As Far Back as Herodotus

Twenty-five hundred years ago, the Greek historian Herodotus
wrote, "Man stalks across the landscape, and deserts follow in his
footsteps."[1] Plato also saw fingerprints from the withering hand
of Man on the land. In *Critias* he wrote that after logging and
goat browsing in the high hills of Attica, "What now remains
compared with what then existed is like the skeleton of a sick

man, all the fat and soft earth having been wasted away, and only the bare framework of the land being left."[2]

Right before and after the time clergyman and economist Thomas Malthus wrote an "Essay on the Principle of Population" in the late 1700s, scientists such as George-Louis Leclerc, Comte de Buffon and Alexander von Humboldt worried about the harm done by swelling swarms of Man. George Perkins Marsh, Abraham Lincoln's ambassador to Italy and Turkey, wrote his path-finding book *Man and Nature* about the scalped landscapes he saw in the Mediterranean. He believed that the downfall of earlier civilizations came from their flaying of the land.[3]

The 1930s to 1960s

Following Marsh's lead in weighing land-blighting by Middle Eastern, Egyptian, Greek, Roman, and North African empires and spurred by the god-awful Dust Bowl of the 1930s (little recalled today it seems), between 1935 and 1955 scientists and conservationists carefully looked at and warned about thousands of years of soil erosion.

In 1935, Yale botanist Paul Sears, one of America's leading scientists, eyed the loss of topsoil in the United States in his book *Deserts on the March*. Writing during the height of the Dust Bowl, Sears asked, "Is the human race digging its own grave in North America?" He went on to warn:

Man has become the sponsor of a biological experiment without known parallel in the history of the earth and its inhabitants. He is the first example of a single species to become predominant over the rest...He no longer accepts, as living creatures before him have done, the pattern in which he finds himself, but has destroyed that pattern and from the wreck is attempting to create a new one. That, of course, is cataclysmic revolution.[4]

Sears saw population growth as the driver behind desertification. In a preface to the fourth edition of *Deserts On the March* published in 1980, Sears told how demographers had earlier guessed that "the population of the United States would stabilize at around one hundred sixty million by 1960."[5] If only it had. It's well over three hundred million today and it could hit eight hundred million by 2100 if we don't do something.

Carl Sauer, the leading geographer of the mid-1900s, wrote in 1938, "In the space of a century and a half—only two full lifetimes—more damage has been done to the productive capacity of the world than in all of human history preceding." He saw it as "a reckless glutting of resource for quick profit."[6]

In 1938, the assistant chief of the United States Soil Conservation Service (SCS), W. C. Lowdermilk, was asked by the Department of Agriculture to make an on-site "survey of land use in olden countries for the benefit of our farmers and stockmen...in this country." For eighteen months Lowdermilk and his fellows roamed through western and southern Europe, North Africa, and the Middle East. The SCS published his report with photographs in a thirty-page bulletin, *Conquest of the Land Through 7,000 Years*. Lowdermilk found "tragedy after tragedy deeply engraved in the sloping land throughout the lands of early civilizations." He ended *Conquest of the Land* with the "Eleventh Commandment" that he had first given in a talk in Jerusalem in 1939: "If any shall fail in this stewardship of the land thy fruitful fields shall become sterile stony ground and wasting gullies, and thy descendants shall decrease and live in poverty or perish from off the face of the earth."[7] If only we had heeded his wisdom then and since worldwide.

In 1948, Fairfield Osborn, President of the Conservation Foundation and a well-known scientist, wrote *Our Plundered Planet*, which also drew on fallen civilizations that had grubbed the wealth out of their lands. Osborn showed how a swiftly growing population was a threat. He warned that the world's human population could double in seventy years. The world population in 1948 was about 2.3 billion.[8] Many brushed him off as a fearmonger. Was he? Well, by 2014 the world's population was well over seven billion: *Over three times as much.* Osborn worried that world population would reach 4.6 billion in 2018. But by 2014, there were over 2.4 billion more people than he foresaw!

Another leading conservationist of the time, William Vogt, wrote *Road To Survival* in 1948, in which he warned, "By excessive breeding and abuse of the land mankind has backed itself into an ecological trap." He wisely brought overpopulation and bad stewardship together as drivers of ecological breakdown. Conservation historian Roderick Nash sees Vogt and Osborn as laying the groundwork for Paul Ehrlich and Garrett Hardin.[9]

About this time, Aldo Leopold wrote in his insightful essay, "Round River," "One of the penalties of an ecological education is that one lives alone in a world of wounds."[10] I believe in saying this, the great conservationist Leopold was mulling over the harm we do to wildlife and wildlands, not just how we gobble raw goods.

Some of the best and toughest thinking about overpopulation was offered in articles and scientific papers in academic journals in the 1950s and 1960s. It's hard to track these down now, but some of them found their way into "environmental studies" anthologies beginning in the late 1960s with Paul Shepard and Daniel McKinley's wonderful stock of papers, *The Subversive Science: Essays Toward an Ecology of Man.*[11] Few books shaped me like this one did. If you want to understand the history of how we talked about overpopulation in the middle of the last century, which was the key time after all, you need to know some of the scientists and their papers squirreled away in academic anthologies like *The Subversive Science, Environ/Mental* (also by Shepard and McKinley) and Roderick Nash's *American Environmentalism.*

In 1955, Tom Dale of the Soil Conservation Service and Vernon Gill Carter of the National Wildlife Federation wrote the most thorough work up to that time of Man's wounding of the land: *Topsoil and Civilization*. After carefully sifting through the archaeology and history of the world's civilizations, they wrote, "The fundamental cause for the decline of civilization in most areas was deterioration of the natural-resource base on which civilization rested."[12]

Today's writers too often overlook the work of Sears, Lowdermilk, Osborn, Vogt, Dale, Carter, and others like them. They come up with cultural or political grounds for the fall of civilizations and don't speak to the perils of population growth and landscalping. In many ways, these older works are still the best for grasping why civilizations slump and crash. Modern scholarship is weak in its lack of knowledge about trailblazing scholarship fifty to one hundred years ago and uppity about highlighting worthwhile writing not in peer-reviewed journals today. As good as some of today's books like Jared Diamond's *Collapse* may be, I still think the older books by our wise elders are more straightforward and should be read first to understand our world.

When *Topsoil and Civilization* came out, wise and learned men (but no women—times have changed, thank goodness) from all over the world gathered for a week in Princeton, New Jersey, to chew over *Man's Role in Changing the Face of the Earth*. The great American geographer Carl Sauer was co-chair along with the free-roaming scholars Lewis Mumford and Marston Bates. A year later, the two-volume proceedings were published.[13] Although little known today, this meeting laid the broad scholarly background for talking about carrying capacity and how we harm Earth. Attendees ran the gamut from mining advocates and other kinds of landscalpers to farsighted conservationists. I find it bewitching that Charles Darwin's grandson Sir Charles Galton

Darwin and Aldo Leopold's son Luna Leopold were there.[14] In an ending session, Darwin said that he was "an absolutely convinced Malthusian."[15] Although he believed that we would not stop population growth, he steadfastly called out to his fellows, "Do not let us be blamed by our descendants for not trying."[16]

In 1956, Shell Oil Company geologist M. King Hubbert predicted that "the peak of crude-oil production in the United States would occur between 1966 and 1972." It peaked in 1970.[17] Hubbert's work gave bedrock to thinking about resource depletion.

So, long before what many believe to be the beginning of today's conservation movement, or of the "environmental movement" in the 1960s, thoughtful scientists and historians were looking to yesterday to understand today. There they found deserts in the footsteps of civilizations. Rutgers biologist David Ehrenfeld, whose book *The Arrogance of Humanism* needs to be read by everyone, wrote, "'Desert-makers' is truly as appropriate a title for humans as 'tool-users.'"[18]

David Brower and into the 1970s

While David Brower was executive director of the Sierra Club, he shoved human population growth into the forefront of the conservation movement when he published Paul Ehrlich's *The Population Bomb* in 1968. In his foreword to the book, Brower wrote:

It was only twelve years ago [1956] that we even suggested, in any Sierra Club publication, that uncontrolled population was a menace. We went far enough to write: "People are recognizing that we cannot forever continue to multiply and subdue the earth without losing our standard of life and the natural beauty that must be part of it... These are the years of decision—the decision of men to stay the flood of man."[19]

In *The Population Bomb*, Paul Ehrlich warned:

> [T]he world's population will continue to grow as long as the birth rate exceeds the death rate; it's as simple as that. When it stops growing or starts to shrink, it will mean that either the birth rate has gone down or the death rate has gone up or a combination of the two. Basically, then, there are only two kinds of solutions to the population problem. One is a "birth rate solution," in which we find ways to lower the birth rate. The other is a "death rate solution," in which ways to raise the death rate—war, famine, pestilence—find us.[20]

Hundreds of thousands of copies of *The Population Bomb* sold. Overpopulation was brought up to the front burner. More than once, Paul Ehrlich was a guest on Johnny Carson's *The Tonight Show*.

In the year *The Population Bomb* came out, leading Italian industrialist Dr. Aurelio Peccei gathered a small worldwide bunch of businessmen and scientists to talk about tomorrow. Out of that meeting grew The Club of Rome, which asked a team of scientists at the Massachusetts Institute of Technology (MIT), led by Donella Meadows, to study exponential growth of human population and industrialization. That work, with early computer models, was published in 1972 as *The Limits to Growth* and ended with a cold-water-in-the-face warning:

> If the present trends in world population, industrialization, pollution, food production, and resource depletion continue unchanged, the limits to growth on this planet will be reached sometime within the next one hundred years. The most probable result will be a rather sudden and uncontrollable decline in both population and industrial capacity.[21]

The Limits to Growth was a key step in understanding how we harm Earth's wherewithal to keep us alive and healthy. Meadows' follow-up study in 1992, *Beyond the Limits,* was a more thorough work, and *Limits to Growth: The 30-Year Update* even more so.[22] These are resource conservation books and don't give much heed to wild things. Even so, it is telling that a study looking only at the well-being of Mankind can come out so strongly on the need to limit growth. One doesn't need to be a lover of wild things to worry about the outcome of the population explosion—to see that there are too many of us.

After David Brower left the Sierra Club, he kept up his work on population with Friends of the Earth (FOE), which rushed *The Environmental Handbook* into print in time for the First National Environmental Teach-In on April 22, 1970. The Teach-In became better known as Earth Day. This mass-market paperback was a collection of new and reprinted articles along with wide-roaming thoughts on how to get out of our overpopulation plight. It didn't beat around the bush; it called for making population stabilization a national policy and giving foreign aid "only to countries with major programs to curb population growth." We need to bring both of these things back to the fore today.

The Environmental Handbook also set as a long-term goal "half of the present world population, or less." In 1970, there were fewer than four billion of us. Some environmentalists and conservationists therefore called for a world population of fewer than two billion humans.

At one of the Earth Day rallies in 1970 there were also warnings of extinction. At the University of Michigan, University of Wisconsin botanist Hugh Iltis cautioned that we were bringing on a mass extinction—and that overpopulation was making it happen.[23]

What a time this was. We have fallen so far. At that time, overpopulation was a plight strongly acknowledged within the radical "ecology" movement.[24] Widespread worry about overpopulation was not "politically incorrect," and neither was earnestly calling for lowering worldwide population, or—my goodness— for giving aid only to countries working to lower their popula- tions. What if such backbone existed today?

Post 1970s

Since the 1970s, there has been a small flood of books about population growth, resource depletion, and carrying capacity. In *Living within Limits* and *The Ostrich Factor,* lion-hearted Garrett Hardin slew the sacred cows of today's beliefs right and left. The Ehrlichs lay out why they rightly think that the population bomb has exploded in their strong and sound book, *The Population Explosion,* which also stands out for its early eyeballing of global warming.[25]

One of the best of the books on overpopulation and the key one for lovers of wild things is *Overshoot* by William Catton, Jr.[26] Another one that stands out for its tough truthfulness and fearless seeking of understanding is *The Spirit in the Gene* by Australian photojournalist Reg Morrison.[27] Wide-thinking biol- ogist Lynn Margulis wrote the foreword, and Harvard's E. O. Wilson blurbed on the back, "Reg Morrison offers varied and often fascinating documentation from ecology, economics, and natural history to portray human history for what it is, a Greek tragedy in which our greatest strengths are no less than our most dangerous flaws."[28] Morrison writes, "The graph of human pop- ulation growth over the past ten thousand years is disturbingly similar to the population graph of an animal entering what we would commonly describe as a plague phase."[29] *The Spirit in the Gene* is an unsettling book.

More recently, a few historical and geopolitical overviews belly up to the bar in their willingness to look at human pop- ulation growth and the shadows where it may lead. *The Human Web: A Bird's-Eye View of World History* by the son-father pair of J. R. McNeill and William McNeill may be the best short overview of world history. Prior to this book William McNeill wrote *Plagues and Peoples,* a trailblazing work that showed how epidemic disease has often steered world history (for example, it was smallpox, not guns, horses, and Spanish military genius, that smashed the Aztec Empire).[30] J. R. McNeill, his son and author of *Something New under the Sun: An Environmental History of the Twentieth-Century World,* is also a top historian.

In *The Human Web,* they see global civilization rising over the last five thousand years as local and regional civilizations slowly spun "webs" of trade, travel, and takeover among one another. Far-flung civilizations had their own kinds of epidemic diseases that became set as populations grew big enough to keep the germs always alive in someone's body. (e.g., about half a million people in one web was needed to keep a pool of measles happy.) Among their host humans, such ills became less deadly as years went by, and adapting human populations climbed. But when webs met and overlapped, diseases killed millions as they flowed into new, unexposed populations. World population growth could not truly take off until Europe, India, China, and lands in between were brought into the same epidemiological world, about 1800 C.E. when "the world's separate webs fused."[31] The great webs weaving together left no big epidemic-naive populations. The McNeills' insightful breakthrough has helped to understand why population growth shot up in the last two hundred years.

A good number of books on the coming oil shortage have come out in the last few years. Richard Heinberg's *The Party's Over* is most sound because he draws on petroleum geologists and doesn't fall into conspiracy theories. He also pops the rosy bubbles of alternative-energy and organic-farming boosters, showing that we've overshot carrying capacity and there are no silver bullets. He writes, "Both leftist and rightist ideologies contain an element of unreality or even denial concerning population and resource issues."[32] Given that a progressive—even countercultural—Canadian publisher, New Society Publishers, published his book, Heinberg is forthright about overpopulation and how immigration drives growth in the United States.

World security expert Michael Klare's *Resource Wars* should ring true with foreign policy realists and those worried about American security. He is more straightforward in looking at how population growth plays in world happenings than are most environmental and conservation leaders. He writes, "The growing demand for resources is driven, to a considerable degree, by the dramatic increase in human numbers." He also gives weight to "the spread of industrialization to more and more areas of the globe and the steady worldwide increase in personal wealth..."[33] He sees most bickering in the world today and tomorrow as "*resource wars*—conflicts that revolve, to a significant degree, over the pursuit or possession of critical materials."[34] He carefully weighs the threat of greater and greater water shortages in hungry lands that have booming crowds and depend on irrigated farming. Climate breakdown now swells an even bigger wave of hunger and thirst toward them.

The late Samuel Huntington, in *The Clash of Civilizations and the Remaking of World Order*, also looked at population growth as a slide to a wobblier world. He wrote that "the Resurgence of Islam has been fueled by equally spectacular rates of population growth."[35] Without population stabilization, even the best of peacemakers may as well part the Red Sea with the wave of a stick. The sad truth is that fast population growth unleashes a chain of outcomes—high unemployment among young men, which leaves them frustrated and unsettled, unable to start their lives and families, and prey to radicals and to hatred of others who seem to have what they can't have.

Lester Brown, founder of Worldwatch Institute and Earth Policy Institute, has long been the foremost thinker about whether the growing world crowd can feed itself tomorrow. His 2004 book, *Outgrowing the Earth: The Food Security Challenge in an Age of Falling Water Tables and Rising Temperatures,* is a wakeup call to all cornucopians. He pulls in the whole puzzle—erosion, withered soil fertility, pricier and dearer fossil-fuel-based fertilizers and herbicides/pesticides, dropping groundwater, drying rivers and snowpacks and mountain glaciers, climatic weirdness, crashing seafood stocks, fatter diets, and population growth—to help readers understand why we are looking at an awfully hungry and unsettled tomorrow.[36]

The Overarching Truth

After sifting through lessons in the dirt, Archaeologist Steven LeBlanc lays out in his landmark book, *Constant Battles,* how our tale has long been about the struggle between neighboring bands over scant resources. No other writer, however, has done better than Edward Abbey in shining a light on the overarching truth:

> *Growth for the sake of growth is*
> *the ideology of the cancer cell.*

The ideology of the cancer cell has dogged followers among economists, politicians, and social activists of the left, liberal, and conservative political spectrums, among radicals and moderates, among corporate CEOs and peasants. Even with the many who have warned us about Man's limits, and even if we realize we are on a cancerous growth path, we humans still have a deep-seated loathing to acknowledge the truths and consequences of limits.

9

THE GREAT BACKTRACK

Unlike plagues of the dark ages or contemporary diseases we do not yet understand, the modern plague of overpopulation is soluble by means we have discovered and with resources we possess. What is lacking is not sufficient knowledge of the solution but universal consciousness of the gravity of the problem and education of the billions who are its victims.[1]
—*Rev. Martin Luther King, Jr., 1966*

Over the last thirty years, there have been many shifts in the conservation, environmental, and resource camps. Maybe the most striking and deep-rooted is that these camps worked hard to spotlight the booming Man swarm in the 1960s and 1970s, yet today overpopulation worry is kicked into the corner and shunned like an old, smelly dog. This is a tectonic shift.

In today's world, overpopulation is overlooked as the mainspring of ecological and social woes. There have been news stories about wretchedness and starvation in Africa for a long while. Most of these reports don't tip a hat to overpopulation as the root (or even a rootlet) or look at how population stabilization and reduction could help lessen the woes. In the fall of 2005 there was much ado about starvation in Niger. Left unsaid about this forlorn land was that the United Nations said it had the highest birthrate in the world. At the time, the beaten-down souls highlighted in the news all seemed to have about nine kids. Could this have had anything to do with why Niger was a hungry wreck? It didn't seem as though any of the reporters were asking.

Likewise, environmentalists in the United States lambaste suburban and exurban sprawl (as they should). But do they acknowledge that over half of sprawl is driven by population growth, that the United States is the only big, wealthy land with third-world growth rates, and that our growth is mostly goosed along by immigration? This head-in-the-sand mood showed itself further in the fall of 2006 when the United States snapped the three-hundred-million-head wire. Environmentalists and con-servationists should have been marching in the streets to warn that we must reduce our population. But even those who should understand that there are limits to population growth mostly overlooked this frightful benchmark.

When environmentalists did say something about it, they seemed to shrug it off as small potatoes. For one, a spokesman for the Environmental Defense Fund said that population growth itself wasn't what was wrong; it was where people chose to live.[2] This is just not true. When we snapped the two-hundred-million wire way back in 1968, scientists and leading anti-war do-good-ers such as Linus Pauling and Jonas Salk put their names on a full-page newspaper ad about this milestone. The ad splashed a few words across a photo of a bouncing, diapered, smiling baby. The words? "Threat to Peace." In smaller type, they explained, "It is only being realistic to say that skyrocketing population growth may doom the world we live in."[3]

At the time in Great Britain, the new Ecology Party (Greens) worked on what a sustainable population would be, Oxfam (the international antipoverty foundation in England) called for zero population growth, and Greenpeace UK was shouting, "Stop at Two." Today, the Greens, Oxfam, and Greenpeace have dropped the population stabilization issue. A once hard-hitting British group, Population Countdown, "worried about alienating funders, became Population Concern and, more recently, Interact Worldwide."[4]

If we are going to keep the wild world, we must deeply and truthfully ask why organizations like these have backed away from the overpopulation fight.

Historian Samuel Hays, in his landmark book *Beauty, Health, and Permanence* wrote that in the 1970s, "It was rather widely agreed that population growth should be limited."[5] Widely, indeed; former President Eisenhower in 1968 said, "Once, as president, I thought and said that birth control was not the business of our Federal Government. The facts changed my mind...I have come to believe that the population explosion is the world's most critical problem." Keep in mind that Ike said this as Vietnam was blowing up in our hands and when the Cold War was about as hot as it got. Three years earlier, President Lyndon Johnson had told the United Nations that "five dollars invested in population control is worth one hundred dollars invested in economic growth."[6] That wisdom should be etched into marble above the main door of the World Bank. A Gallup poll in 1976 showed that in North America, "eighty-four percent said that they did not want more people in their country and eighty-two percent not in their community."[7] Today we seem happy to crowd into an endless sardine can. In 1976, the U.S. population was a little over two hundred million; as of 2014 it is reaching 318 million and continues to climb.

Why the Retreat?

In their two papers, "The Environmental Movement's Retreat From Advocating U.S. Population Stabilization" and "Forsaking Fundamentals," environmental scientist Leon Kolankiewicz and journalist Roy Beck give a most thorough look at why U.S.

environmental and conservation bodies have shunned population quandaries.[8] William Ryerson, president of the Population Media Center, wrote in *Wild Earth* in 1998/99 how political correctness led to the international backing-off on overpopulation.[9] These researchers are unsparing truth seekers. Kolankiewicz and Beck see five drivers behind the "American environmental movement's retreat from population advocacy": (1) Dropping Fertility; (2) Anti-Abortion Politics; (3) Emergence of Women's Issues as Priority Concern of Population Groups; (4) Rift Between Conservationists and New-Left Roots; and (5) Immigration Becomes Chief Growth Factor.[10] In his weighing of how international population stabilization work was torpedoed and left to sink, Ryerson spotlights lowering of U.S. fertility rates, the Catholic stand against contraception and abortion, the feminist shift to pronatalism, and how the Reagan Administration dropped U.S. leadership.[11] There are even deeper roots having to do with Man's nature. And then there are the warnings about the wrong things.

Fertility Rate Drop in Wealthy Countries

Although the population had been growing by frog-leaps in the West since 1800 and the world over after 1900, soldiers coming home after World War II lit the fuse of the population bomb in the United States and other wealthy countries—the Baby Boom. The Total Fertility Rate (TFR—the average number of children per woman) for American women in the 1950s was 3.5; 2.1 is the TFR to keep a population stable. By 1969, President Richard Nixon warned, "One of the most serious challenges to human destiny in the last third of this century will be the growth of the population. Whether man's response to that challenge will be a cause for pride or for despair in the year 2000 will depend very much on what we do today."[12] You can knock Nixon for other failings, but when it comes to concern about overpopulation, he was a great, farsighted statesman brimming with wisdom.

Also in 1969 in her commencement address at Mills College, Stephanie Mills said, "The most humane thing for me to do is to have no children at all."[13] Stephanie was thrust into national celebrityhood for her selfless oath. She was not alone in her feelings, as I and others of our generation had no children by choice too. Many others chose to have one or two children.

As a result, something striking happened: "[T]he birth rate in the United States dropped dramatically...By 1973, the fertility rate had fallen to replacement level." In 1975, the TFR was only 1.7. The news media blasted headlines like "Population Problem Solved" and "U.S. Arrives at Zero Population Growth."[14] However, it was a sweeping misunderstanding that getting to replacement-level fertility meant that we'd hit zero population growth. "Population momentum" keeps the population climbing for "up to seventy years after the replacement-level fertility is reached," write Kolankiewicz and Beck.[15] And it was only wealthy countries that gained replacement-level fertility. Despite this fact, many folks in the United States and other wealthy lands believed the population threat was over. Even many environmentalists and conservationists believed it and shoved population to the back burner.

Nonetheless, lowering the birth rate in the United States, Europe, Japan, and elsewhere was an awesome deed. In 1975, a stabilized U.S. population of no more than two hundred fifty million was in our grasp. But we've let that hope fall through our fingers. Without taking strong steps now, in 2100 the U.S. will have a population that is over 700 million—three times the number at which our population could have stabilized had we not stumbled since the late 1970s. As we shall see, we failed because we didn't pay enough heed to what was happening in Washington, D.C. with immigration legislation at the time.

Anti-Abortion Politics

The Catholic Church sneered at worry about population growth owing to its belief that contraception is a sin. When the pope finally allowed the rhythm method in 1930, journalist, satirist, and critic H. L. Mencken wrote, "It is now quite lawful for a Catholic woman to avoid pregnancy by a resort to mathematics, though she is still forbidden to resort to physics or chemistry."[16] With the Supreme Court's *Roe v. Wade* ruling in 1973 making abortion lawful, the Catholic Church heaped up wrath about "baby killing" to their spurning of family planning. Catholics got into bed with their once foes, fundamentalist Protestants, in an antiabortion storm that helped lead to today's authoritarian right.[17] William Ryerson writes, "Recognizing that concern with population growth was one of the reasons many people supported legalized abortion, the Right to Life movement evolved a strategy to cast doubt on the existence of a population problem." It was their hold on Ronald Reagan that led him to end the international leadership of the United States on population stabilization at the 1984 U.N. population conference in Mexico City.[18] The old men of the Catholic hierarchy swore that those worried about overpopulation were anti-Catholic. The Church also set out "to disprove that rising population size had anything to do with deterioration of natural or human environments or the ability of poor countries with rapidly-growing populations to develop economically."[19] Unlike Nixon, at least on population, the popes and cardinals have been shortsighted old men, deaf to the cries of millions of hungry babies headed for slow deaths or crippled lives.

The ugliness of the Catholic nobility's damnation of birth control was laid out by the head of Catholics for a Free Choice, Frances Kissling, in an op-ed for the *Baltimore Sun,* where she brought forth outlandish statements from Catholic leaders. A Ugandan Cardinal, Emmanuel Wamala, told Catholics in Africa that it would be better for women to get AIDS from their husbands than to use condoms. The president of the Pontifical Council of the Family, Cardinal Alfonso Lopez Trujillo, told

BBC that HIV can go through a condom (it can't). And Kissling writes that a priest told her on CNN's *Crossfire* that "it was worse to lose your soul and go to hell because you used a condom to prevent AIDS than to die of AIDS."[20] Maybe the Catholic hierarchy would have gotten more upset with wayward priests had the priests used condoms with young altar boys.

Emergence of Women's Issues as Priority Concern of Population Groups

Some social activists became upset by population stabilization work in China and India, both of which were growing by leaps and bounds in the 1970s. By yelling about "coercion," such do-gooders killed family planning talk at the third U.N. population conference in Cairo in 1994. There they flipped the goal from putting the brakes on population growth to the empowerment of women. Family planning experts, writing in the British medical journal *The Lancet,* say, "The recommendations of the Cairo Conference replaced the hitherto dominant demographic-economic rationale for family-planning programmes with a broader agenda of women's empowerment and reproductive health and rights." Funding for international family planning dropped. By 2000, the drafters of the U.N.'s Millennium Development Goals pretty much did away with worry about overpopulation and overlooked family planning.[21]

Feminist and human-rights groups were the big dogs in this shift. Outsiders from such outfits were even brought in to take over the population committee of the Sierra Club. As a Sierra Club board member and member of the conservation governance committee at the time, I challenged the population committee's draft goal as the empowerment of women. I tried to get them to understand that this is scrambling means and ends and that the organization's goal must be population stabilization and then reduction. Empowering women may be a key path to that goal, but it is not the goal itself. I won for a while but soon left the Sierra Club board because of its back-off on population.

Kolankiewicz and Beck write, "Now centered in a feminist rather than environmental mission, many population, family planning, and women's groups would support no talk of stopping growth or reducing average family size because that implied restrictions on what they considered a universal right of women to choose their number of children entirely free of the merest hint of official or informal pressure."[22] In essence, the family planning/population movement showed itself to be blind to limits to growth—and to the worth of other Earthlings. To say that women have the right to have as many children as they want is much the same as saying that people have the right to as many gas-guzzling, land-ripping SUVs as they want. Except it is worse. Either way, it says that it is OK for anyone to have selfish whims that ransack wild things. As with so many things, we humans can scramble rights with irresponsibility.

Even the once-tough Zero Population Growth (ZPG) chickened out and changed its name to "Population Connection." The new acronym—PC—has a telling meaning.

Schism between the Conservationist and New-Left Roots of the Movement

Just as in other political ideologies, some on the left are at odds with conservation. Population is one of the flash spots. In the Earth Day era, socialist environmentalists like Barry Commoner shunned the thought that population growth was behind environmental plights. However, anti-establishment bunches, such as the Berkeley Ecology Center, were strong on the need to lower population then. Internationally, leftist environmentalists sidelined overpopulation early on—the 1972 United Nations Conference on the Human Environment in Stockholm, Sweden, did not deal with overpopulation. For one thing, social justice leftists felt that talk about overpopulation blamed the world's poor for the environmental plight; instead, they said, we should target high living in wealthier countries. They were also upset by China's one-child policy and India's widespread sterilization as raids on freedom. Some of those writing on international overpopulation have underlined these so-called "human-rights wrongs" for why work on overpopulation was dropped by international agencies. China was able to keep its one-child policy going and slowed its population growth markedly. India, after the assassination of Indira Gandhi, shoved its program into a back room. The upshot has been that China has "sharply reduced child malnutrition" and only "seven percent of its children under five are underweight." We'll see if these numbers remain low; in late 2013, China approved the relaxation of its one-child policy. Sadly India, however, has an "epidemic" of childhood malnutrition, with 42.5 percent of its kids under five being underweight.[23] There are other drivers behind deep hunger in India (a World Food Program report in 2009 said that India had two hundred thirty million hungry people, or one-quarter of the world's whole), but bungled population work is a leading one. India is now set to become the world's most populous country. In doing so, it will gain a landslide of woe.

Immigration Became the Chief Cause of U.S. Growth

Recall that by the mid-1970s, TFR in the United States, as in Japan and many European countries, had come down below 2.1 children per woman. Our population was set to even out. We had clipped the wires on the population bomb—in the United States, at least. But then we threw our win away, without wilderness and wildlife lovers, including me, understanding what was happening.

Kolankiewicz and Beck write, "When most Americans began to focus on U.S. growth in the 1960s, immigration was an almost insignificant fraction of growth…At the very time that American fertility fell to a level that would have allowed population stabilization within a matter of decades, immigration levels were rising rapidly…By the end of the 1990s, immigrants and their offspring were contributing nearly seventy percent of U.S. population growth."[24]

While Americans of reproductive age were doing their share to stabilize growth, Congress cut them off at the knees by greatly raising immigration. Kolankiewicz and Beck point out that, "If immigration and immigrant fertility had been at replacement level rates since 1972—as has native-born fertility—the United States would never have grown above two hundred fifty million. Instead, U.S. population passed 273 million before the turn of the century." Unless we do a quick u-turn, our population will shoot past four hundred million before we know it. Former Colorado governor Richard Lamm, a Democrat, liberal and conservationist, asks, "Given present realities, why do we want our children to face an America of four hundred million people?"[25] Why, indeed?

In the forty years after 1925, immigration into the United States ran at about two hundred thousand a year. Since immigration law "reforms" in 1965, yearly immigration has leapt to over one million—or five times what it had been earlier.[26] I can't help but think that only a year after the federal government passed the Wilderness Act in 1964, it opened the floodgates to a new threat to wilderness—exponential growth. What makes the 1965 immigration law so bitter is that the 1964 Wilderness Act put population growth at the forefront of threats to wilderness:

In order to assure that an increasing population, accompanied by expanding settlement and growing mechanization, does not occupy and modify all areas within the United States and its possessions, leaving no lands designated for preservation and protection in their natural condition, it is hereby declared to be the policy of the Congress to secure for the American people of present and future generations the benefits of an enduring resource of wilderness.

Statement of Policy, Section 2(a),
The Wilderness Act, PL 88-577.

Here is where things get nasty. Because immigration is now the driver of population growth in the United States, the herd mindset of political correctness stops any unruffled, thoughtful talk about population in this country. Merely acknowledging that immigration is behind population growth gets one accused of racism. This only became so in the 1990s—in 1989 the Sierra Club's stand was that "immigration to the U.S. should be no greater than that which will permit achievement of population stabilization in the U.S."[27]

Kolankiewicz and Beck show how immigration stopped conservationists from working to freeze population in the United States. The way environmental and conservation clubs see themselves as a wing of progressivism makes them fear to nettle leftist friends and leaders of racial-advocacy outfits by acknowledging what more immigration will lead to. And when social activists took over some (most?) of the environmental and conservation funding community, more and more foundations ended funding to groups that spotlighted immigration and overpopulation.

Loss of Overpopulation Leaders

Although pro-growth advocates elbow people away from worrying about population growth, it has been the bludgeoning of Paul and Anne Ehrlich, the late Garrett Hardin, Richard Lamm, and other population-freeze proponents that has undercut good population work among conservation and environmental clubs. Many leaders like Wisconsin Secretary of State Doug La Follette and former Senator Gaylord Nelson have long spoken out on the threat of overpopulation and worked for population stabilization, but the politically correct crowd has undercut freeze work. With Nelson's death in 2005, leftist cornucopianism has become even stronger.

Popular Belief that with Ehrlich vs. Simon—Simon Wins!

After the drop in American, European, and Japanese fertility rates, many people believed that growth was no longer a worry. Thanks somewhat to the scenarios which have not happened (yet) of widespread starvation leading to world war in *The Population Bomb*, people think that overpopulation is not something to fear. The unfortunate popular thinking that Ehrlich was "wrong" has shifted the minds not only of right-wing economists but conservationists and environmentalists as well.

Affluence Is Worse Than Population

Recall the I=PAT formula—Impact=Population x Affluence (Consumption) x Technology. Those who lean toward political correctness within the environmental and conservation crowds think that unbridled consumption among the wealthy has more to do with ecological Impacts than does the Population boom among the poor (or anyone). It's not how many people there are as much as how much they have and how high on the hog they live. This is where we get matchups such as one American having as much Impact as seventy Nigerians or thirty-five Indians. This A versus P match is no small thing, and I wrestle with it in the next chapter.

Digging Deeper

Let's dig a little deeper to understand why we backed off on overpopulation. Maybe we have been asking the wrong thing, which has been, "Why have society at large and the environmental and conservation teams backed off from forthright work on population growth?" What we should ask instead may be: "Why did people for a short while between the end of World War II and the mid-1970s worry about population growth?" In other words, maybe the lackadaisical feeling of today is the everyday mood and the worried days of the population movement were the oddity.

It also boils down to Man's history. For generations we have believed that it is our reproductive destiny to want and love babies. Even though more people are having no children by choice in today's society, from a social and cultural imperative standpoint, not wanting offspring is still seen as odd.

Then there is tribalism. Archaeologists and primatologists show how we humans and our forebears have worked to kill off nearby bands since at least our last shared forebear with chimpanzees five million or more years ago. In the age-old struggle for expansion and goodies, one's own band needed to be stronger than the neighboring bands. The quickest path for being mightier than your neighbors was to have a bigger gang of young male spear-chuckers. We see this wanting of population overlordship playing out in the immigration wars today in Europe, North America, and Australia. Throughout the world, leaders of ethnic (tribal) immigration outfits flatly say they want more immigration of their bunch for greater political might that will lead to takeover. Socio-political foes of wide-open immigration warn that the traditional American (or European) ethnic blend is being swamped by the ethnic makeup of immigrants. This worry in the United States comes from blacks and non-Hispanic whites. I also hear it from native New Mexicans of Spanish and Native American backgrounds about those coming from Mexico and Central America. We also see the war club of more bodies being swung today in Israel-Palestine, in Sunni-Shia-Kurd Iraq, Tibet, Bolivia, Ukraine, Darfur, Rwanda-Eastern Congo, and Fiji. We also see it in those who believe that by keeping our population high, the United States can go on being *the* world power.

Julian Simon further wins the day against Paul Ehrlich because he offered uplifting words against dire warnings. Our attraction to optimism may well be part of our human nature. People want to believe that everything is going to be OK, that we are going to keep making headway in every way, that each generation will have a better life than the one before—even when all the warnings flash and screech, "No!"

Optimistic cornucopians shun carefulness as a social pathology. David Ehrenfeld sheds light on why this is so: "The motive for their constant insistence on being optimistic and 'positive' is simply the converse of this; optimism is necessary for those who are attempting the impossible; they could not continue to function without it."[28] Were they to face the dark pit before us, they would lose their will to live. They would have to come nose to nose with their madness. This they know. To keep the dread from their minds, they curse the truth tellers who attempt to pop their fantasies.

Eugene Linden wisely writes, "Widespread optimism has always been a good indicator that disaster is around the corner."[29] His book, *The Future in Plain Sight,* is a careful, thoughtful look at likely tomorrows. Then couple this with humans' tendency toward shortsightedness. Psychological experiments and watching others show that more of us than not are shortsighted and do not think about the long run.

Then there are those who are not in the fantasies driven by optimism and who do see the big picture but decide to give up. For example, I can almost understand conservationists and environmentalists who, after chewing on all of this, end up feeling that population stabilization and reduction is hopeless. Their backtracking results from convincing themselves that their sweat is better spent on other issues facing our overpopulated world.

10

POPULATION OR AFFLUENCE—OR TECHNOLOGY?

Take, for example, a hypothetical American woman who switches to a more fuel-efficient car, drives less, recycles, installs more efficient light bulbs, and replaces her refrigerator and windows with energy-saving models. If she has two children, the researchers found, her carbon legacy would eventually rise to nearly forty times what she had saved by those actions.[1]

—*The New York Times*

Remember John Holdren's and Paul Ehrlich's scientific formula, (I) Impact = (P) Population x (A) Affluence (resource consumption) x (T) Technology, or I=PAT? There are those who believe that lowering Affluence is the way to live within carrying capacity and lower our Impact. Others believe that Technology can do much of the wonderwork to keep Impact down while we grow Affluence and Population. They think that Technology can raise Affluence and cut Impact, so we don't need to give heed to Population. Is Technology the answer to our woes? Let's take a closer look.

What Technology Does to Impact

In *Constant Battles*, archeologist Steven LeBlanc shows us the way Technology works in I=PAT.[2] Technology can hike carrying capacity, letting both Population and Affluence rise. When we get down to it, this is the true saga of Man going back not only through the fifty thousand plus years of *Homo sapiens* but even further back to earlier *Homos*, as LeBlanc shows so well in *Constant Battles*. While Technology can stretch carrying capacity, it does not soften Impact. It shoots up Impact. Again, this is the true tale of Man. A technological step "forward" raises our carrying capacity. Population and Affluence then grow until they come up against the new carrying capacity. Bad things happen until there is a new Technology breakthrough, which again raises carrying capacity. And so on. But a higher carrying capacity for Man means we have a greater Impact on wild things.

This cycle has gone on longer than there have been *Homo sapiens*, at least back to *Homo heidelbergensis*, the forebear for both Neanderthals and us. It may even go back to *Homo erectus* or *ergaster*. Let's see how it *might* have played out.

For a long while, our forerunners were kept small by predation. We were cat food. Likely pretty darn easy cat food. With more skillful rock throwing, stone chipping, and then wielding of wooden spears and mastery of fire, we steadily became tougher prey, and our population slowly grew. When *Homo sapiens* as Cro-Magnons came to Europe, their better tool kit, which made them better big game hunters, raised their carrying capacity over what the Neanderthals likely had. Better social organization, microliths, sewing awls, fish hooks, atlatls, bows and arrows, bringing dogs into our bands, and other hunter-gatherer steps "forward" all drove the cycle. Technological breakthroughs raised carrying capacity, grew Population and Affluence, and had greater Impact on wild things.

The cycle jumped to a new, much higher plateau with settled life, grain storage, weaving, pottery, and domestication of wheat, beans, goats, sheep, pigs, and cattle. Top human paleontologist Niles Eldredge of the American Museum of Natural History writes, "The stunning growth of human population after the invention of agriculture can mean only one thing, namely, that the primordial limits to…growth were demolished. We did not simply get better at wresting a living from ecosystems: We actually stopped doing that…in favor of agriculture."[3] Then came copper, bronze, and iron, irrigation, wheels, and cities.

If I may be so bold as to tinker with the Ehrlich's and Holdren's equation, this true saga of Man plays out as: Higher Technology = higher Carrying Capacity = higher Population and Affluence = higher Impact on wild things: HT=HCC=HP+HA=HI.

Nearly everyone, even those in the population stabilization movement, seems to see the plight of population growth only as a modern problem, or at most one that popped up with the rise of the first states. In *Constant Battles* Steven LeBlanc and his wife, Katherine Register, blow that Noble Savage wish out of the water. In it LeBlanc lays out evidence from primatology, biological anthropology, human paleontology, archaeology, history, and ethnology to show that the unending bloodshed and wars between and within human groups come from overshooting carrying capacity resulting from population growth.

There have never been human bands that lived long in ecological harmony with their surroundings or that were sustainable. As their numbers grew, they overtaxed the land and wild resources around them, which led to scalping their habitat and to the likelihood of hunger and starvation. When this happened, resource fights began with neighbors, and wars waged over many years to wipe out the competition for resources in short supply.

At each step on the ladder of growing cultural complexity, new technologies boosted carrying capacity of the land (and sea), which led to bigger populations and deeper ecological wounds. Since the evolution of behaviorally modern Man some fifty thousand years ago and our spread out of Africa into the rest of the world, this has been our history. No matter how cultures "progress" through the stages from foraging bands to tribes to chiefdoms to kingdoms to the modern state, we keep on overshooting carrying capacity even though technological advances at each step raise carrying capacity. We have now reached the end of that road. There are so many folks gobbling so much that our waste of carbon dioxide, methane, soot, and other greenhouse gases is shifting the make-up of the atmosphere, thereby disrupting climate and acidifying the seas, which kills off coral reefs and other ocean life. With seven billion people and counting, we have overshot the carrying capacity of the atmosphere and the oceans to take in and hold harmless our waste.

Once again, we may have reached the end of the cycle. A crash—bigger than all the cycles before—lies head.

The Ecological Footprint

Among the people who work to cut Impact, there has long been a split between those who think we need to freeze and then lower Population and those who think we need to cut back on wastefulness (Affluence). The truth is we need to freeze and cut *both* Population and Affluence. Without lowering Population, cutting back on Affluence can't do the job.

We've termed a deft way to frame Impact as one's "Ecological Footprint." However, it has the same limitation and weakness as carrying capacity in that it weighs only our Impact on Earth's wherewithal to support Man in the manner to which we've become accustomed. In *From Big to Bigger,* a great report that looks at mass immigration and the Ecological Footprint, Leon Kolankiewicz defines the latter this way:

The Ecological Footprint is a measure of aggregate human demands, or the human load, imposed on the biosphere, or "ecosphere." When all is said and done, the human economy, all production and consumption of goods and services, depends entirely on the Earth's natural capital—on arable soils, forests, croplands, pasturelands, fishing grounds, clean waters and air, the atmosphere, ozone layer, climate, fossil fuels, and minerals—to perform the ecological services and provide the materials and energy "sources" and waste "sinks" that sustain civilization.[4]

Those who see Affluence/consumption as the key wield the Ecological Footprint as a yardstick for lowering their Impact through lifestyle shifts. These shifts include:

- ❖ Drive less/get a higher mileage car/take the bus/bicycle/walk
- ❖ Buy food grown nearby/eat organic/grow your own/eat lower on the food chain
- ❖ Make your house more energy efficient/live in a smaller house/live with others

All of the above steps and like ones are good. We need to take them or some of them as much as we each can. Americans can lower their footprints by trimming fat—but as Colorado State philosophy professor Philip Cafaro and wildlife biologist Winthrop Staples warn in their landmark paper, "The Environmental Argument for Reducing Immigration to the U.S.," they aren't going to give up too much. Japanese and Western Europeans live well but one-on-one are thriftier with energy and have smaller footprints than do Americans and Australians. Cafaro and Staples say we should cut our consumption to where Japanese and Europeans are, but "barring universal enlightenment or dire catastrophe," cutting back to how Mexicans live or—good heavens—Nigerians or Bangladeshis, "aren't live *political* options."[5] In other words, we can bring our per person footprint down, but not nearly enough for *generous sustainability*, which Cafaro and Staples frame as "(1) creating societies that leave sufficient natural resources for future human generations to live good lives; and (2) sharing the landscape generously with nonhuman beings."[6]

It follows then that we have no choice but to freeze then reduce our numbers. Otherwise, we will lose more and more other kinds of Earthlings from our landscape. Anyone who thinks we can double or triple U.S. population without wiping out wildlife and scalping our last wildernesses, lives in a fool's paradise—not in the real world where we either will or will not keep the other Earthlings hale and hearty in our shared neighborhoods.

Here is some good research and analysis that strongly show that to make our footprint smaller, we must lower our population.

Sprawl

In the U.S., urban and suburban sprawl tramples and kills wildlife in a big way. For example in the twenty years between 1970 and 1990 in the one hundred biggest U.S. urban hubs, more than nine million acres of wildland or cropland was lost to new sprawl. In their study, *Weighing Sprawl Factors in Large U.S. Cities*, Leon Kolankiewicz and Roy Beck took a thorough look at the one hundred biggest-in-acreage cities in the U.S. to find the key driver for each's sprawl—population growth or the trend to bigger houses and yards. Stock wisdom holds that high-flying lifestyles drive sprawl and that population growth plays a small role, if at all. But that's not what Beck and Kolankiewicz found.

Kolankiewicz and Beck identified two mainsprings: *per capita sprawl* and *population sprawl*. Per capita sprawl comes from bigger homes and lots, and is tweaked by tax, zoning, and transportation policies, while population sprawl comes from more bodies. Looked at overall, the two were nearly even for how much sprawl they drove, but population growth came out somewhat higher.

For years the mantra in the West has been: "We don't want to be another Los Angeles." We've thought of L.A. as the king of sprawl. But as Kolankiewicz and Beck write about L.A., "No city in America may be a better model of attempting to restrain sprawl by channeling population growth into ever-denser settlements, both in the urban core and throughout the suburbs." Believe it or not, since 1970 land-use restrictions have made the greater L.A. metropolitan area the most thickly settled landscape in the U.S., with only 0.11 acre per dweller. The suburbs of New York City are "only sixty percent as dense as those of L.A." Nonetheless, Los Angeles has sprawled—from population growth.

Kolankiewicz and Beck delved into the one hundred high-est-sprawled cities in the U.S. from 1970 to 1990 and calculated the percent rise or loss of population and the acreage for each dweller. Then they figured out the growth of each city in square miles and then by percentage of the earlier land area. From that, they "apportioned" the percentage of sprawl to either population growth or per capita land consumption.

Detroit had the eighteenth most acres, a population loss of 6.9 percent, and a 37.9 percent growth in one-on-one land consumption. So in apportioning its sprawl, zero percent is from population and one hundred percent is from the jump in how much land each homeowner took. Los Angeles has the sixth biggest acreage, a population gain of 36.5 percent, and an 8.4 percent *drop* in per capita land consumption. Apportioning its sprawl gives us one hundred percent from population and zero percent from growth in how much land each dweller took. My hometown of Albuquerque is forty-fourth in the U.S. for land spread, a population gain of 67.1 percent, and an 18.1 percent bump in one-on-one land consumption. When apportioned, 75.5 percent of sprawl is from population growth and 24.5 percent from greater household land footprint.

Overall, Kolankiewicz and Beck find that from 1970 to 1990 50.9 percent of the sprawl results from population growth and 49.1 percent from per capita land consumption. What they find is as sharp as broken glass—"smart growth," even when it does as well as it has in Los Angeles, cannot stop sprawl by itself. The takeaway:

Only by also freezing population growth can sprawl of new suburbs onto rich cropland and wildlands be stopped.[7]

The reality—none of the Seven Ecological Wounds can be healed without freezing and then lowering population. With an endlessly booming population:

We will not be able to lower greenhouse gas emissions.
We will not be able to gain clean air and clean water
for people to breathe and drink.
We will not be able to make sure that the other
Earthlings who came into the twenty-first century with
us will last until the twenty-second.
Welcome to the Real World.

Jevons' Paradox

For some time we've been told that if each of us cut back on energy, water, food, appliances, cars, and miles driven, the overall weight of these things on Earth would ebb, and raw goods would last longer. But a handful have known the truth—that this is just not so.

At the end of the Civil War (1865), an economist named W. Stanley Jevons wrote a book about coal and how it was being used more efficiently in steam engines. In *The Coal Question* he wrote,

"It is a confusion of ideas to suppose that economical use of fuel is equivalent to diminished consumption. The very contrary is the truth." Over one hundred years later, two economists, Daniel Khazzoom and Leonard Brookes, also wrestled with "Jevons' Paradox." In his article, "The Specter of Jevons' Paradox," Jeff Dardozzi writes, "They argued that increased efficiency paradoxically leads to increased *overall* energy consumption." As more researchers have looked into this paradox, it has become more unforgiving. Earthscan, a publisher of books and journals on climate change, sustainable development, and environmental technology, published an entire book on it. *The Jevons Paradox and the Myth of Resource Efficiency Improvements* looks at the history of this puzzling truth and studies that prove it.

Dardozzi writes, "The second effect resulting from efficiency improvements is that when you save money you usually spend it somewhere else in the system of production, and that translates into increased energy and resource consumption." Take my hometown of Albuquerque, where in older neighborhoods residents are nagged to cut water use. But cutting back on yard watering, baths, and toilet flushes doesn't mean Albuquerque sucks less water from the ground or the Rio Grande. It means that there is now "more" water for new home building on the growing West Side of town or for new industrial plants. In other words, people who have lived in a house for fifty years should let their peach trees die from no watering so a builder can have it for new houses and home buyers being lured to Albuquerque. As Blake Alcott, an ecological economist, writes about this twist worldwide, "[G]iven global markets and marginal consumers, one person's doing without enables another to 'do with.'" Or said another way, we in the U.S. can cut way back on our driving, but what oil we don't burn will be gladly taken by all the new car owners in India and China.[8]

Jevons' Paradox also plays out when it comes to lighting. It shot down Sandia Labs researcher Jeff Tsao's once hopeful prediction. In 1999, Tsao wrote a white paper that showed if conventional light bulbs were swapped for solid-state bulbs, "The worldwide amount of electricity consumed by lighting would decrease by more than fifty percent and total worldwide consumption of electricity would decrease by more than ten percent." Ten years later, though, Tsao discovered Jevons' Paradox and how it applies to lighting. *Albuquerque Journal* science writer John Fleck reports, "As lighting became more efficient—from candles and kerosene to gas and then electric lights—people wanted to have more light, rather than to use less energy."[9]

With Jevons' Paradox at work, what should we be worried about? Engineers coming up with straightforward, cheap, endless, clean wellsprings of power. Why? Nothing would wreck the wild Earth quicker and more thoroughly than clean energy too cheap to meter. This would also let population zoom even higher.

What's the way out of Jevons' Paradox? Freeze population, then bring it down.

Carbon Legacies

Many folks want to make their footprint smaller. However, many people don't realize the biggest way to make a footprint smaller boils down to having fewer or no children. Research by statistics professor Paul Murtaugh and Michael Schlax, an oceanic and atmospheric science professor at Oregon State University show that children greatly swell the acreage of one's carbon footprint. *The New York Times* reports, "Take, for example, a hypothetical American woman who switches to a more fuel-efficient car, drives less, recycles, installs more efficient light bulbs, and replaces her refrigerator and windows with energy-saving models. If she has two children, the researchers found, her carbon legacy would eventually rise to nearly forty times what she had saved by those actions."[10]

Forty times.

Murtaugh and Schlax published their research in the peer-reviewed journal, *Global Environmental Change*.[11] To find the "carbon legacy of an individual," they looked at how many children, grandchildren, and so on one has and worked out a "weighting scheme" giving each offspring's Impact as a fraction of relatedness. In their words, "That is, a parent is responsible for one-half the emissions of their children, one-quarter the emissions of their grandchildren and so on." They also calculated how much one could cut one's carbon output from six lifeway shifts and found it was about 486 metric tons of CO_2 in a run-of-the-mill American woman's lifetime. But the carbon legacies of each birth foregone under three emission scenarios come out to between 9,441 and 12,730 tons. In other words, not having a child cuts a woman's carbon legacy twenty times more than six lifeway shifts. Murtaugh and Schlax have essentially found that not having a kid dwarfs all the other "green" lifeway shifts put together.

Murtaugh and Schlax have shown well the weight of P in I=PAT. Murtaugh noted that their "calculations are relevant to other environmental impacts besides carbon emissions—for example, the consumption of fresh water, which many feel is already in short supply."[12] Their path can be followed for studies weighing Population and Affluence and other ways we wound the living Earth.

These studies and analyses agree that we can't lower Impact by only lowering Affluence. Population is the big dog in I=PAT. It likely has a greater share of I=PAT than does Affluence. Think of it this way—Americans have the biggest Affluence Footprint per capita of any people in the world. Any population growth in the U.S., then, is growth of these big Affluence Footprints. Population growth in the U.S. does more harm to the world than population growth anywhere else because of our over-big Affluence.

The world cannot afford more Americans.

11

THE THORNY ISSUE OF IMMIGRATION

Immigration to the U.S. should be no greater than that which will permit achievement of population stabilization in the U.S.

—Sierra Club population policy, 1989

We started down the thorny road of immigration in the chapter, The Great Backtrack. Now let's get into the thicket, starting with this truth—population growth in the U.S. from any driver, be it too many births or more immigration than out-migration, and whatever the background, economic rung, or homeland of immigrants, harms the quality of life in the U.S. and hurts wild things in the U.S. and worldwide.

We lovers of wild things need to worry about immigration to the U.S. and take the talk back to biodiversity carrying capacity and how more men, women, and children mean fewer wild things. The answers to the following questions get at some hard facts:

Is population in the United States growing?

Yes, it is, at about three million per year. The first Census of the independent U.S. in 1790 found a total of about three million Americans. We are now adding that *every year*. We can look at population growth with this formula:

$$(B_c + I_m + B_i) - (D + M) = G$$
(Births to citizens+Immigration+Births to immigrants)–
(Deaths+out-Migration)
= Population Growth

By 2050, the Census Bureau forecasts that the U.S. population could be growing between two and two and a half million per year. Demographers think that, far from slowing down on the way to freezing, yearly U.S. population will keep growing with no end in sight. That is unless there is a downward shift in net migration. The Census Bureau shows "net international migration" at 794,000 to 884,000 in 2015 and 1.2 to 1.6 million in 2050. This is almost a fifty percent jump. Chew on that. Unlike me, many of you reading this may be alive in 2050. And keep in mind that U.S. Census Bureau forecasts are nearly always low.

Where is the growth coming from?

Population growth in the U.S. flows out of three springs:
1) Net immigration (lawful and unlawful)
2) Net natural growth among U.S. born (births to citizens)
3) Net natural growth among foreign-born (births to immigrants)

Note that only number two would be happening without net immigration. Numbers one and three must be wed to show the full net weight of immigration.

Philip Martin, a professor at the University of California, Davis, puts immigration in perspective since World War II: "The United States admitted an average of two hundred fifty thousand immigrants a year in the 1950s, three hundred thirty thousand in the 1960s, four hundred fifty thousand in the 1970s, seven hundred thirty-five thousand in the 1980s and over one million a year since the 1990s."[1] No wonder our population has been growing.

According to a 2012 Pew Research and Demographic Trends report, despite recent declines in birth rates to immigrants in the U.S., "foreign-born mothers continue to give birth to a disproportionate share of the nation's newborns, as they have for at least the past two decades." The report also indicates that the 2010 birth rate for foreign-born women was nearly fifty percent higher than the rate for U.S.-born women. When it comes to U.S. population growth:

Population projections from the Pew Research Center indicate that immigrants will continue to play a large role in U.S. population growth. The projections indicate that immigrants arriving since 2005 and their descendants will account for fully eighty-two percent of U.S. population growth by 2050. Even if the lower immigration influx of recent years continues, new immigrants and their descendants are still projected to account for most of the nation's population increase by mid-century.[2]

What is the up-to-date population of the United States?

You can find the U.S. population clock at https://www.census.gov/popclock/. There you will also find "components of population change," including the time it takes to add one "international migrant" to the U.S. and the time it takes for a "net gain" of one person to the U.S. population. The day I wrote this, one international migrant was added every thirty-eight seconds, and the net gain of one person occurred every fifteen seconds. And on June 4, 2014, the U.S. population was 318,177,475. Go to this website and check out the most up-to-date numbers.

If the United States had adopted the Sierra Club 1989 proposal on immigration in 1989, what would be our population today?

In 1989, the Sierra Club held the position that immigration to the U.S. should be no greater than that which will permit achievement of population stabilization in the U.S. At that time, the U.S. population sat at roughly two hundred fifty million. Had the U.S. done something twenty years ago, our population may have never broken the three hundred-million wire.

Under today's trends of legal and illegal immigration, what will be the population of the United States in 2050?

In Pew Research Center's 2014 FactTank, it projects the U.S. population to grow by eighty-nine million residents from 2010 to 2050, and reach 401 million by 2050.[3] The U.S. Census Bureau predicts the numbers will hit 420.3 million by 2060.[4]

What would the United States 2050 population be if immigration were capped today so that in and out migration matched (The Sierra Club 1989 policy)?

The Census Bureau zero-net migration projection for 2050 (grounded on 2009 population projections) is 323,000,000— seventy-eight million fewer than the mainstream forecast of 401 million with immigration.[5]

What will the U.S. population be in 2100 if we don't at least slow immigration?

If net (not gross) immigration is kept at no more than 1.5 million bodies a year, U.S. population in 2100 will be over seven hundred million. However, some bills in Congress could goose lawful immigration to more than two million a year. If such "reforms" become law, U.S. population could flood to over eight hundred fifty million in 2100.[6] This is why the immigration boosters don't talk about numbers. These numbers are mind-blowing.

THE UNITED STATES IN THE YEAR 2100

Today's U.S. population	318 million*
Yearly Net Immigration	1.5 million
Net Immigration in 2066 Kennedy/Bush bill	over 2 million
U.S population in 2100 with 1.5M immigrants yearly	over 700 million
U.S. population in 2100 with 2+M immigrants yearly	over 850 million
U.S. population in 2100 if we freeze immigration	*about 330 million*

*http://www.census.gov/popclock/, September, 2014

These numbers show the weight of immigration. With population growth figures like these, how many more tons of greenhouse gases will be churned out every year? How many wild acres will be taken over by housing, highways, parking lots, shopping malls, farmland, coal strip mines and mountaintop removal, oil and gas drill pads, and road/pipeline webs? What about total energy use? New nuclear plants and nuclear waste with nowhere to put it? Total water use? How many more dams, miles of irrigation canals and pipes, and groundwater pumping? How many acres of homeland and foraging land for other Earthlings (wildlife) will be taken over by all the new men, women, and children in the U.S.? Why are we doing this to our country? To the wild things living here?

This is what we should be talking about when we talk about immigration.

Immigration to the United States Raises the Overall World Footprint

People come to the U.S. not to keep the standard of living they had in their country of origin but to get the standard of living of the everyday American. Because the American standard of living is built on the highest squandering of energy and other raw goods in the world (other than for a Gulf sheikdom or two or three), each American has a greater Impact than others do on the goodness of life for wild things. In a nutshell:

We in the United States cannot afford more Americans.
Others in the world cannot afford more Americans.
The wild things of the United States
cannot afford more Americans.
Wild things worldwide cannot afford more Americans.

Population growth in the United States does not just have a crushing Impact on wildlife and wilderness in the U.S. Our standard of living, which is kept high by grubbing up wildlands all over Earth for raw goods, has an overwhelming Impact on wild things worldwide. The more people coming to the U.S. for that standard of living not only threaten other Earthlings that dwell here but other Earthlings that dwell all over the Earth.

Immigration from poor lands with lower footprints than the U.S. makes for more folks with sky-high American footprints. This is one side of immigration that hasn't been closely looked at until recently. Philosophy professor Philip Cafaro and wildlife biologist Winthrop Staples looked at the ten countries that send the U.S. the most immigrants and then lined up their total ecological footprints.[7] The following table lays it out.

AVERAGE ECOLOGICAL FOOTPRINT OF U.S. CITIZENS AND 10 LARGEST IMMIGRATION SOURCE COUNTRIES, 2003 (GLOBAL HECTARES PER PERSON)

Source Country	% of U.S. Immig. Pop. (2000)	Total Ecological Footprint
United States	---	9.6
Mexico	29.8	2.6
China/Taiwan/H.K.	4.5	1.6
Philippines	4.4	1.1
India	4.0	0.8
Cuba	2.8	1.5
El Salvador	2.7	1.4
Vietnam	2.5	0.9
Korea	2.3	4.1
Canada	2.2	7.6
Dominican Republic	2.0	1.6

Source: Philip Cafaro and Winthrop Staples, "The Environmental Argument for Reducing Immigration to the United States," *Backgrounder*, Center for Immigration Studies, June 2009, 13.

The U.S. has a total ecological footprint of 9.6 hectares (nearly twenty-five acres) per person. These global hectares are worked out with a mathematical formula crafted by John Holdren, co-creator of I=PAT, former president of the American Association for the Advancement of Science (AAAS), and (since 2009) Director of the Office of Science and Technology Policy under President Barack Obama.

The 9.6 hectares each American needs are scattered all over the world. The total per capita ecological footprints for the ten countries that send us the most immigrants go from 7.6 for Canada to 0.8 for India. Mexico, which sends us about thirty percent of all our immigrants, has a 2.6 hectares (6.5 acres) per person footprint. So when Mexican immigrants or their children gain an every-day American life (not when they first come to the

U.S.), each will have goosed up their footprint by seven hectares. Leaving aside Canada, immigrants from the other nine of our top ten immigrant-sending countries will swell their total ecological footprint and the footprints of all of their offspring "by one hundred percent to one thousand percent or more." Mexicans will raise their footprint by three hundred fifty percent if they come to the U.S. and gain our fat life.[8] Each immigrant to the U.S. raises his/her footprint and by doing so raises the worldwide footprint of Man.

Why is Immigration So Thorny?

The population growth numbers from immigration are amazing. Increases in ecological footprints—unsettling, to say the least. So why is the idea of reducing immigration met with such scorn? It starts with too much talk about *immigrants* instead of *immigration*.

Many pro-immigrationists sketch those wanting less immigration as the bad guys of American history—nativists, racists, Ku Klux Klanners. Those who want to stop or slow immigration express concerns about terrorists and the dilution of American culture. Both sides trot out economics, national security, and human rights to uphold their beliefs. Neither side talks about population growth, much less how growth in the U.S. is harmful to wild things worldwide.

About six years after the Sierra Club came out with its thoughtful and fair 1989 immigration policy, most of the Club leadership turned against caps on immigration. I was on the national Board of Directors at the time. Why did this flip happen, and how did it happen so quickly? For one thing, in 1994 California had a bloody political fight over ballot Proposition 187 that would have kept illegal immigrants from getting state-supplied social services. Whatever the arguments for or against Proposition 187 might have been, the election was deeply divisive in the state with outlandish charges and distortions being thrown back and forth. The California Sierra Club took a public position against the proposition. Some of us protested that whatever the feelings of individual Sierra Club members, the Club should have officially stayed out of the fight with no position on it. Proposition 187 came only five years after the good Sierra Club immigration policy, but it shifted the ground within the Club, markedly in California. It put many Sierra Club activists close to ethnic activists who led the fight against Proposition 187. On the other side, *some* of those working for the proposition were hardcore nativists with a load of right-wing ties.

After the Proposition 187 fight (it passed but was found unconstitutional by a federal court), the Sierra Club in California found itself in a new political landscape. It seemed Club leaders did not want to be linked with the others calling for immigration caps after the nasty Proposition 187 election. As the Club became seen as a feather in the progressive wing of the Democratic Party, it felt at home with those against immigration caps. Leading Mexican-American politicians in California aligned with Sierra Club issues in the state and Club leaders did not want to risk their backing by being thought of as anti-Mexican in any way. There was also a $100,000,000 (!) gift from a billionaire who told Carl Pope, Sierra Club Executive Director at the time, that he would cut the Club off if it said anything against immigration.

Nonetheless, in 1998 some old-time Sierrans put up an initiative in a Sierra Club election to go back to the 1989 policy. They were seen as right-wing "outsiders" trying to take over the Club. However, those who endorsed this initiative were anything but outsiders. Those for the return to the 1989 Immigration Policy included well-known conservation leaders, professors, authors, political leaders, and foundation leaders from a range of ethnicities.

At this same time, The Wilderness Society, a leading American conservation organization took a fair, thoughtful stand on population policy, which dealt with "the consequences of population growth to our wild lands." It said, "As a priority, population policy should protect and sustain ecological systems for future generations." And to "…bring population levels to ecologically sustainable levels, both birth rates and immigration rates need to be reduced."[9] Unfortunately, The Wilderness Society didn't do anything to boost its policy, but at least it undercut the Sierra Club leadership's mudslinging at those backing immigration caps. With only slight updating, this 1996 policy should be taken by all conservation groups today worthy of the name.

When it comes down to it, conservationists and environmentalists stopped working to cap immigration—even if it was the only way the U.S. could freeze its population—because they did not want to be linked in any way with the right-wing, nativist, anti-immigrant crowd. The way to deal with this, however, is not to give up on working to cap immigration but to shift the framing of immigration policy. We need to speak more from the question of *how many* not *who*. To get out of the thicket, we need to help people understand that cutting immigration is not anti-immigrant and not tied to nativism or racism, but tied directly to our ecological future.

If You Don't Back Capping Immigration, What Do You Back?

It comes down to this—if you don't back capping immigration to the U.S., you back our population growing to over eight hundred fifty million by 2100.

What else do you back?

Cafaro and Staples put it this way. If you support continued mass immigration into the U.S., you support:

- ❖ Drastically increasing America's human population
- ❖ More cars, more houses, more malls, more power lines, more concrete and asphalt

❖ Less habitat and resources for wildlife; fewer forests, prairies, and wetlands; fewer wild birds and wild mammals

❖ Replacing these other species with human beings and our economic support systems [10]

If you back this kind of population growth, you also say yes to making it nearly hopeless to keep wildlands and wild things on the landscape.

The U.S. Census Bureau estimates that 37.6 million foreign-born people lived in the U.S. in March 2010. This population includes naturalized citizens, non-citizen legal immigrants, and undocumented immigrants. Take note that 37.6 million is an estimate; the actual number is more than likely higher because millions of undocumented immigrants live in the U.S.[11] Contrast this to 1970, when only 9.6 million immigrants lived in the U.S. Even in what we think of as the great heyday of immigration to the U.S., from about 1920 to 1930, there were never more than 14.2 million immigrants in the U.S., says the U.S. Census Bureau. When it comes to immigration, we are wildly out of kilter today.

Lowering the immigration rate will in no way go against American tradition. And even if it did go against our tradition, so what? Not all of our traditions grant other Earthlings a home on the landscape. We don't slaughter buffalo anymore or dump DDT into our rivers. We've brought back wild things—wolves, river otters, hawks—that were once earnestly murdered. In the same light, we need to make a big shift in our immigration policies to keep and bring back the wildlife of North America.

The Ecological Argument for Immigration to the United States

I've heard only one argument from the pro-immigration side that rests on ecological grounds. Back when I was on the losing side of the fight over immigration policy in the Sierra Club in the mid-1990s, Carl Pope put it this way to me: For the sake of biodiversity, letting Guatemalans come to Los Angeles is better than them hunting wildlife and hacking out new *milpas* in the backwoods of Guatemala.

This argument seems to be grounded on the following beliefs:

❖ Biodiversity has more worth in Guatemala than in Southern California.

❖ The growing population in Guatemala will go to wild-lands in Guatemala if they can't come to the U.S.

❖ Someone in Guatemala will have a heavier footprint on wild things than someone in Southern California.

Are these beliefs grounded or do they come from clever argument? First of all, it looks at only Guatemala and Southern California. Such thinking does not weigh the footprint gap between a Californian and a Guatemalan on the rest of the world. Moreover, it is akin to what I sometimes hear from those who want more logging of the National Forests—Any less logging in the U.S. will only lead to more logging elsewhere in the world where logging is less regulated (if at all) and where biodiversity may be greater. I've heard the same song from nearly every other U.S. resource-extraction industry fighting checks on its plundering. It's all self-serving, ill-founded blather to rip off raw goods from the public lands. In truth, we in the U.S. take more care logging (though not enough) thanks to conservationists than do other countries, and by doing a better job here we can show others how to do better. If we ransack our big woods though, what trustworthiness do we have for showing other countries how to take better care of their forests? If we overfish within our exclusive economic zone, how can we tell others to not overfish their stocks?[12] And if we let our population boom to once-unthinkable crowds, how do we talk to other countries about cooling their population growth?

But, insofar as Guatemala goes, we're being an overflow pond for reckless overbreeding in Central America and Mexico (and for the Philippines and Africa and...). So long as we offer that overflow pond, there is less need to lower birth rates in those countries (birth rates have come down but not enough for stabilization). About ten percent of the adult population of Guatemala already lives in the U.S. and most adults in Guatemala would like to come as well, according to polls. Who can blame them? What needs to happen instead? They need to stay in Guatemala and make it better.

The World Bank reports that in 2012, the total fertility rate for women in Guatemala was 3.8 children.[13] Family planning is not working in Guatemala, somewhat owing to the might of the Catholic Church. Guatemala can keep having such a high and thoroughly unsustainable growth when the U.S. continues to serve as an overflow pond for too many births. If we quit being the relief valve for the baby swell in Guatemala, births would have to come down. Checks sent from Guatemalans working in the U.S. to family back home also keeps heavy breeding going there. Researchers need to look closely at how such remittances keep high births propped up in the third-world countries.

Philip Cafaro wisely wrote to me, "Opponents of immigration reduction often argue that overpopulation is a *global* problem, so we should pursue global solutions for it. But this overlooks the fact that solving the global problem depends on individual *nations* getting their own population houses in order. The U.S. can contribute to this by first getting our own house in order, by ending our own growth. And second, by taking away the safety valve that allows Mexicans, Guatemalans, Dominicans, and others to keep breeding irresponsibly. This *is* the main way we can contribute to a global solution to global overpopulation."

If we are an overflow pond for Meso-America, why not for the whole world? Where do we draw the line? *When* do we draw the line?

The least painful time to draw the line is now. Not when there are twice as many of us in the U.S. (or three times as many people in Guatemala). Truly, the best time to have drawn the line was in the 1980s before immigration to the U.S. boomed. We flopped and we flopped thoroughly. But that does not let us off the hook to do better today.

Is there something wrong with thinking that wild things in the U.S. are less worthy than those in Guatemala? I think so. In temperate zones worldwide, the wildlands of Southern California are matchless when it comes to a manifold neighborhood of life, but they are beset by the grinding and rending roll of building. Southern California has more threatened and endangered species than any landscape of like size in the U.S., but for Hawaii. Besides, *this is our home,* and we have a responsibility to love and keep its wildlife and wilderness. There is something deeply wrong and wickedly unpatriotic with thinking that the U.S. should be a sacrifice zone for the rest of the world.

As we know, a newcomer to Southern California will have a much greater worldwide ecological footprint than someone living in Guatemala City. And booming crowds in Latin American countries are not heading to the backwoods to hack out new *milpas* but are pulling up stakes and heading to the cities. So, when we come to the end of this debate, it is not whether it's best for Guatemalans to come to Los Angeles or to cut down the rainforest, it's whether they go to Guatemala City or to Los Angeles.

Again, it shakes down to—Earth cannot afford more Americans.

Put that bumper sticker on your car—or bicycle.

Take an Ecological Stand on Immigration

A 2014 poll conducted by NumbersUSA indicates that more people in the U.S. want to see drops in immigration. As *The Washington Times* reports on the poll findings, "Currently, the

U.S. allows in about one million legal immigrants a year, but sixteen percent said that should be cut to five hundred thousand, another seventeen percent wanted to see it drop to one hundred thousand, and a full twenty-six percent said they want to see a halt to all legal immigration. By contrast, just sixteen percent said to keep it at one million and only eleven percent wanted to see an increase to two million." Most respondents said, "Legal immigration should be cut at least in half." NumbersUSA found deep "concern over jobs and a reticence to add more immigrant labor to the market."[14] Keep in mind that these responses come without knowledge about the upshot of ongoing immigration— from 318 million in the U.S. today to four hundred million or more in 2050 to potentially eight hundred and fifty million in 2100. If those mind-blowing numbers were bandied about, how would thoughts on immigration shift even more?

We also shouldn't automatically think that Latinos want more immigration. In a 2009 poll, Zogby International found that most Latinos in the U.S. were not behind more immigration nor were they for some kind of "amnesty" for those here unlawfully. Fifty-six percent of Latinos thought immigration was too high, with only seven percent saying it was too low. Fifty-two percent backed "enforcement to encourage illegals to go home," while only thirty-four percent supported "conditional legalization." The authors of the poll say, "The overall findings of this poll show a significant divide between the perception that minority voters want legalization and increased legal immigration and the reality, which is that they want enforcement and less immigration."[15]

What's the larger reality? Unless we cap immigration, U.S. population will more than double by 2100. A swelling population will continue to leave an ever-growing environmental wake. And without capping immigration to the U.S., we cannot freeze— much less reduce—population growth. Ultimately, we need to cap immigration for the sake of wild things in America and everywhere.

Facing this reality means taking an ecological stand on immigration. We need to demand answers from the federal government on how immigration will make our footprint bigger and heavier—and deadlier. We must stand up loudly and call for a full environmental impact statement (EIS) on immigration policies. Lawsuits need to be filed requiring such a study. We need to lobby members of Congress to introduce a bill requiring an EIS. A thorough environmental impact statement on immigration to the U.S. might be the most important EIS ever done. It is the one way to bring all the facts into full public debate.

12

STEPS TO CAPPING IMMIGRATION TO THE UNITED STATES

This is not to excuse the fact that they either came to this country illegally, or overstayed a visa. As I've said many times, I think illegal immigrants, once detected, should be detained and deported. I just don't see the need to demonize them in the process.[1]

—*Ruben Navarrette, Jr.*

This quote by Ruben Navarrette, Jr., an op-ed columnist for the *Albuquerque Journal* and other newspapers, gives good political advice—and ethical guidance. It's the path I take in this chapter.

Understanding Immigration

To either slow or cap immigration to the U.S. (and other wealthy countries), we must take a keen look at the makeup of immigration. First, we need to ask how immigration today shakes out as lawful and unlawful. Then unlawful immigration can be further shaken out into those who break the law by sneaking over the border and those who come in lawfully on a timed visa and then stay illegally after the visa's time is up. Philip Martin, a professor at the University of California, Davis whose field is migration, writes, "The number of unauthorized foreigners peaked at 12.2 million in 2007, fell by almost one million during the recent recession and may have increased again with economic recovery."[2]

Unlawful immigration is a problem, but lawful immigration is way, way too high, also. If all the heed goes to unlawful immigration, we never get around to asking about whether there is too much *lawful* immigration. If we care about overpopulation in the U.S., we must sweep the border spotlight over to the flood of lawful immigration as well. So not only do we need to shift the talk away from the immigrants themselves to the ecological impact of population growth from immigration, we need to look at unlawful *and* lawful immigration. Too much talk about unlawful immigration keeps us from talking about lowering lawful immigration, which we must also do to stabilize population in the U.S.

The need to cut immigration boils down to how the footprint of Man and carrying capacity harm wild things. The more of us there are, the more this happens. So think about this again:

Had the United States taken up the Sierra Club immigration policy in 1989, the U.S. likely would have already stopped growing at below three hundred million, or, at worst, been set to stop soon at no more than 325 million.

Because we did not, that footprint has mushroomed, and we've surpassed carrying capacity. Our population is flying to undreamed-of heights. Why do folks keep wanting to come to the U.S. to live and work? For a better life—one that is more out of harm's way, one that has better likelihood of making enough to live well for oneself and one's offspring. Philip Cafaro brings up a key, if touchy, side of why folks immigrate: "Often, it is because they and their leaders have failed to create decent societies, where people treat one another with respect and where society's economic resources, however large or small, are shared out reasonably fairly." What holds people back from coming to the U.S.? It means leaving family and the life they know. Leaving means dealing with the unknown; it means gambling with one's life and happiness.

People choose to leave their homeland mainly because they believe they will have better breaks in their new setting. The things that go into making up people's minds to leave home fall into three fields—how bad it is in their homeland, how easy it will be to get to the other land, and how much better they think the other land will be. If we want to slow or shut down immigration to the U.S., we need to come at lawful and unlawful immigration in all three fields.

Field One: Make the United States Less Beckoning

The following steps in Field One do three things: (1) put immigration into overall population policy; (2) end job hopes for illegal immigrants; and (3) encourage all who are in the U.S. unlawfully to go home voluntarily.

Oppose any raise in immigration level.
Make the Sierra Club 1989 Immigration Policy
the law of the land.
Oppose any kind of amnesty or "line jumping"
for those here unlawfully.

The 1989 Sierra Club policy or something like it should become the law of the land for immigration. Cafaro and Staples argue that "we should limit immigration into the U.S. to the extent needed to stop U.S. population growth." This is pretty much the same thing as in the Sierra Club policy. Cafaro and Staples say this will "eventually lead to zero population growth" since the U.S.'s Total Fertility Rate (TFR: the number of births an average woman in a given nation will have in her lifetime) is 2.06 and a 2.1 TFR is "replacement rate."

Such legislation would likely bring lawful immigration down to two hundred thousand a year or less, much as it was before 1965 when we blew the lid off immigration numbers. With such a lower number, the U.S. can be much more choosy about who we allow to apply for entry. Just as we could have stopped growth by 1980, so can we do it today.

Better track visitors.
Send home all who are here unlawfully.
Make hiring unlawful immigrants a felony.
Give employers a way to check status of job seekers.

If people coming in on a timed visa know they will be found and sent home if they overstay and that such law breaking will keep them from being let into the U.S. again, they will be less likely to linger. If employers can easily check at no cost whether job seekers are here lawfully or not, and if they know they will be hit with heavy fines or jail time for hiring immigration outlaws, they will be less likely to hire those who live here unlawfully. We must make it not worth anyone's while to hire immigration outlaws for anything—from factory work to yard work. The only way we can do this is to make lawbreaking hurt.

If those who have slipped into the U.S. unlawfully or lingered past their lawful time know that they will have a nearly hopeless time finding work and that they will be caught, sent home, and banned from ever coming back, even as a tourist, they will be less likely to do so. Those already here can be encouraged to voluntarily leave by a free trip home and no future penalty of being banned from ever coming back.

The federal government already has built a workable, effective system called "E-verify." Philip Cafaro writes, "E-verify is now highly accurate and has proven its ability to cut back drastically in the numbers of illegal workers. Tens of thousands of employees [have] used this system…we should make its use mandatory across the U.S. After all, we (U.S. taxpayers) have paid for it, and we…should get its benefits." Either by federal or state law, all employers should be required to use E-verify, which is jointly run by the Department of Homeland Security and the Social Security Administration. Employers who don't use E-verify or who knowingly hire those here unlawfully must know they will get the book thrown at them in fines and jail time and will be banned from government contracts in the future. Top executives and board members should be in the dock when their plants hire unlawfuls. All government agencies must share knowledge quickly and work together. Agencies should have good sweeteners to work together and get penalized when they don't.

Now is a good time to push immigration caps because immigration from Mexico has taken a big drop thanks to the lack of jobs in the U.S. In August 2009 *The New York Times* reported, "Census data from the Mexican government indicate an extraordinary decline in the number of Mexican immigrants going to the U.S." The drop is twenty-five percent or 226,000 fewer people. Jeffrey Passel, a senior demographer at the Pew Hispanic Center, said, "If jobs are available, people come. If jobs are not available, people don't come."[3] Let's make it unerring, then, that "jobs are not available" to those here unlawfully.

Now is also a good time to limit immigration, since so many Americans are out of work. With unemployment at officially at 6.7 percent, and unofficially even higher, many citizens are desperate for a job. As a 2014 NumbersUSA survey found, a majority of Americans have big concerns about adding more immigrant labor to the market.[4]

If you think any of these ways of making the U.S. less beckoning seem unfair, find out how other countries approach this.

For example, without a passport, visa, or driver's license sneak into Mexico, Guatemala, Philippines, China, Nigeria, Pakistan, India, or another country from which the U.S. gets immigrants. Try to get a driver's license. Try to get a job. When you get out of prison, come back and tell us how awful it is in the U.S.

Field Two: Make it Harder to Get into the United States

Have better checks at airports and for those seeking visas. Allow only accredited schools/universities to issue I-20 documents for student visas.

I do not want tourists, students, scientists, researchers, meeting-goers, speakers, and performers to find it harder to come to the U.S. I would like it to be smoother for such guests to come to the U.S. We should be a welcoming land, open to meeting folks from all over the world and happy for them to see America.

I do, however, want to make it harder for anyone to get into the U.S. unlawfully or to live here unlawfully.

Those coming to the U.S. with a visa by air should have to show their return ticket. Use of that ticket should be tracked so that if it isn't used by the expiration date of their visa, their return ticket will be forfeited and the visitor put on the list for known illegal aliens.

Unaccredited, even fly-by-night "schools" and "colleges" handing out I-20 documents to supposed "students" so they can get student visas have operated as an ongoing immigrant loophole. Such schools then do not watch either attendance at classes or overstaying visas. Only accredited, honest-to-goodness schools should be allowed to give I-20s.

The Department of Homeland Security and the Border Patrol must work better with land-managing agencies, follow management guidelines for wilderness areas and na-tional parks, and obey the Endangered Species Act and other conservation laws.

An Environmental Impact Statement (EIS) must be done before more border barriers are built. Barriers in place must be modified to allow wildlife passage.

I encourage you to check the Defenders of Wildlife immigration policy report, "On The Line: The Impacts of Immigration Policy on Wildlife and Habitat in the Arizona Borderlands" and its website to learn about the plight of wildlife near the border.[5] Smugglers or would-be immigrants do much of the harm to the wildlands and wildlife of the U.S.-Mexico borderlands. Overall, the need to heavily patrol and fortify the border with Mexico will mostly fade if we take three other steps discussed in this chapter: (1) Dash all hope of finding a job or any other way of making a living by those here unlawfully; (2) Reform NAFTA and agricultural policies so that Mexican farmers, big and little, are not driven out of business by U.S. exports of cheap, subsidized corn, chicken, and other products to Mexico; and (3) End the War on Drugs so that Mexico has a better chance of stopping drug smuggling and building a safer, more honest society.

Field Three: Make Homelands Better Than Going to the United States

Help cut birth rates in lands sending immigrants to the United States.

When the U.S. and other wealthy lands serve as overflow ponds for mushrooming Man swarms from hungry or jobless lands, they foster more births in the poor lands. If there were no overflow ponds for the growing throngs, births likely would fall in the homelands. And if the smarter, better-schooled, go-getting folks who now come to the U.S. and other wealthy lands had to stay home or go home after getting graduate degrees, they would use their skills to make things better at home.

As a key step to stem the flow of immigration, the U.S. and Canada need to target family planning efforts to help those countries now sending us the most immigrants, lawful and unlawful, such as Mexico, the Philippines, El Salvador, and Haiti. Europe and Australia need to do likewise. A top goal for the U.S. should be to help bring those countries down to replacement level fertility as soon as can be done. All kinds of carrots and sticks should be offered to promote this goal.

Help job growth in lands sending immigrants.
Make more microloans in lands sending immigrants.

Why do people leave their homelands for big, loud Western cities where they may be treated badly? Because life in the homeland seems without hope. Helping to make better paying jobs in poorer lands would do more than tough border enforcement to keep likely immigrants home. The countries sending us the most immigrants should be at the top for help by the U.S. Instead of hiring unlawful immigrants to work in chicken processing plants in Arkansas, build a plant in Mexico that pays well. Had we spent the billion-plus dollars to build jobs in Mexico and elsewhere instead of the border wall we would have done more to slow immigration—both lawful and unlawful. Money now spent for border barriers would be better spent on making jobs in Mexico and Central America and for helping farmers stay on their lands and compete with crop sales at home and internationally. Microloans can help small business owners lift themselves up. It has worked amazingly well in Bangladesh, where Muhammad Yunus and the bank he founded, Grameen Bank, has granted thousands of small loans to poor people. Yunus won the Nobel

Peace Prize for his work to establish the microcredit movement across the developing world. Along with birth control and fair food trade, microloan work like this would help keep more folks in their homelands.

Reform NAFTA, world trade, and farm support to help hungry lands.

Wealthy countries unwisely and unfairly play hardball with third-world countries on agricultural trade, thanks to arm-twisting from their agribiz lobbies. The non-profit organization, Defenders of Wildlife, says that "since the late 1990s, massive increases in exports of heavily subsidized U.S. corn to Mexico under the North American Free Trade Agreement have reportedly resulted in large displacements of Mexican farmers."[6] This is only one crushing upshot out of scores from the reckless, uncaring food trade strategy of rich countries. Not only is world food trade unjust and unfair, it spawns many poor farmers who cannot even feed their children anymore and who then struggle to get to the U.S., Europe, and Canada.

By propping up their farmers and agribiz industries with unfair food trade, the U.S. and other wealthy countries do four things: (1) undercut and monkey wrench farmers in the third-world countries, (2) keep poor lands in the mire of wretchedness, (3) add to overall hunger in the world, and (4) push immigration to North America and Europe. The unfair food trade we shove down the world's throat ends up doing us great harm because it drives mass immigration. Helping poor farmers in poor countries have a fair shake at their home market and the world market could do much to cap immigration—as well as lift up farmers in the third-world countries and help poor countries better feed their own.

Insofar as Mexico goes, we undercut Mexican farmers and others from earning a living at home, and then we spend untold dollars to keep them from coming north to find work. These policies not only backfire but they are mean and coldhearted, too. We need to help corn farmers in Mexico make a good living, not help agribiz in the U.S. wreck corn farming in Mexico. A thorough, wide-sweeping Environmental Impact Statement needs to be done on U.S. immigration policy that would weigh this tangled mess. And NAFTA needs to be thoroughly redone to help farmers in Mexico.

A 2007 article in *The Washington Post* went into depth about how NAFTA has screwed up things down on the farm in Mexico. Mexican farmers cannot compete with subsidized U.S. corn, chicken, and whatever is now being shipped to Mexico. NAFTA has cheated and harmed farmers in Mexico and driven a rush of out-of-work farmers north over the border. The article ends with a quote from Lorenzo Martin, president of the Tepatitlan Poultry Farmers Association and head of a big poultry farm: "If there are corn subsidies in the U.S. and none here, we're dead. If the U.S. starts selling things extra cheap outside the U.S., then it won't just be small farmers and individuals who will be leaving. It will be people like me."[7]

We could cut back immigration from Mexico more by reforming NAFTA and otherwise helping Mexican farmers be competitive than by walling the border. It's hard to blame folks for sneaking across the border when we are giving them the shaft economically. If more of us who want to cap immigration on ecological grounds howled more about NAFTA and other economic unfairness, we could get more people to understand the harm immigration does.

Stop the bungled "War on Drugs" folly.

Were historian Barbara Tuchman still alive, she could write a follow-up to her *The March of Folly* book on the woodenheaded

"War on Drugs." Lands like Mexico and Central American countries becoming so-called "failing states" without public security or economic hope create a big shove for heavy immigration to the U.S. Once-growing middle classes are crumbling. Much (most?) of this woe comes from the War on Drugs. The winners are the drug lords in Mexico, Columbia, the U.S., and other countries.

The grounds for stopping the War on Drugs could fill a dump truck. Maybe the strongest is that Mexico and other countries cannot have fair, open, law-abiding, workable civil governments and safe streets and neighborhoods for their citizens so long as narcoanarchy wields its deadly might. The *Christian Science Monitor* reports that this fear of crime is behind the wish of many Mexicans—including the middle class and wealthy—to come to the U.S. One-third of all Mexicans, or thirty-five million folks, would like to leave for "el norte," says a Pew survey.[8] Philip Cafaro has asked immigrants from Mexico why they came to the U.S., and writes, "Invariably, they spoke of 'corruption' and the fact that a poor man or woman cannot make a good life in their countries."[9]

More than any other thing, stopping the War on Drugs and treating marijuana, cocaine, and other drugs the same as alcohol and tobacco would slow immigration into the U.S. from Mexico and farther south. The crooked, underhanded setup in Mexico could begin to clean itself up. Citizens would be safer in their homes and towns in Mexico. There would be more work in Mexico and thereby less need to go north for work. The power and wealth of the drug cartels and *Zetas* would go up in smoke. And more law enforcement in the U.S. would be freed up for immigration and making sure those unlawfully here can't get a job.

One of the nastiest things happening in California national forests, parks, and other public lands are marijuana plantations. No longer in little plots gardened by back-to-the-land hippies, backwoods marijuana growing is now big, sophisticated, deadly, and harmful to wildlands and wild things. Many of the plantations are run by big narco gangs from Mexico with full-time farmers from Mexico on them. They have well-laid-out irrigation networks, utilize heavy fertilizers, spread pesticides, and poach wildlife for food and see them as "pests." Narcoanarchy rumbles not only in the backwoods of Mexico and Columbia, but also in California. And such "farms" have started some of California's worst forest fires.[10] Ending the War on Drugs would be the end of these wounds on our public lands.

A full, thorough environmental impact statement on the War on Drugs would show what a mistake U.S. drug policy is and would peg scores of woes and harms done by it.

Three big steps need to be taken:

1) Mexico should legalize marijuana and cocaine, and regulate and tax them as it does alcohol.
2) The U.S. Federal government should decriminalize marijuana and cocaine, and allow their regulated import.
3) States in the U.S. should regulate and tax marijuana and cocaine as they do alcohol and tobacco. Growing marijuana should be treated like growing tobacco or the ingredients for alcoholic drinks. (Colorado and Washington have done this; other states are watching to see how it works out.)

I know a few things about drug abuse. My brother started selling marijuana in his college dormitory and went on to importing hundreds of pounds from Mexico. He died of a heroin overdose when he was thirty-three years old after more than a decade of burglary and ripping off his family (our mother, cousins, aunts and uncles, and me) to support his habit. Had we a wiser policy on drugs then, I think he would have done much better. Indeed, I think fewer young folks in the U.S. would abuse marijuana and cocaine if they were legal as is alcohol. Without the highly dollar-wasteful War on Drugs, there also would be much more money to treat addicts and abusers.

Let me be straight about helping to make life better in Mexico and other lands now sending immigrants to the United States. The steps I've outlined above could help make things better and give some folks more hope and better lives. But I do not share the dreams of the poverty-ending crowd that poor, overpopulated countries can be flipped into wealthy countries. I don't blame the U.S. for all the world's problems and don't blame only wealthy countries for the poverty and corruption of third-world countries. The people, educated classes, and leaders of nations have to take responsibility for making their own lands better. They need to take the responsibility to balance their population with the natural ability of their land to produce food and a decent living for all. There are fields, such as world agriculture trade, where wealthy countries need to change so that farmers in third-world lands can stay on their farms and compete to produce food in their country and on the world market. But in other areas, the need for responsibility lies with citizens of each country. Highly educated people from third-world countries now working in the West need to go home to India, Pakistan, Africa, or wherever and make their homelands better.

Overpopulation is at the bottom of why people immigrate and why wretchedness holds sway over much of the world. In 1946, the year I was born, Mexico had about twenty million people. In 2010, it had almost 121 million. Mexico's population has grown more than six times in sixty plus years. Predictions forecast that Mexico will hit over 156 million by 2050. And Honduras? In the 1940s, it had just over one million people. By 2010 the population had risen to almost eight million. Forecasts predict that by 2050, it will have almost thirteen million—or thirteen times what it had in 1940s.

This kind of population growth is the plight of these and many other countries.

And the sorrow.

The United States boosts more population growth when we serve as an overflow pond for Mexico and Honduras. Instead, the U.S. would do far better to lift Mexico and Central America—our neighbors—to the top of our foreign policy work and to do everything we can to work with them to stabilize their populations.

What we do or don't do today will build the world of tomorrow. No other thing than capping or not capping immigration will have such far-reaching and overwhelming consequences for the U.S. and the world. If we do something now, we can make a U.S. that will never have more than 325 million people. But if we do nothing, then we build a U.S. that within the lifetime of a child born today will have twice the population of today—over six hundred million—or even nearly three times the population of today—to eight hundred million.

What kind of U.S. do you want? What we do today will reflect what kind of America the Earth has to bear in 2100.

13

WHAT WE CAN DO

How do we get the general body politic to accept the truth?
—Garrett Hardin (1972)

So. More of our kind is bad for all living things. What do we do about it? First off, we need to understand that much of what we need to do is not hard. In both the technical and public health worlds, we know what to do. We have the tools. We have the skills. We have the worldly background. We have cut the birth rate in many lands.

We need to keep doing what we have done with family planning and get serious about overpopulation education to get people to see the burning needs. It is not hard; it only needs will. Will, however, is missing now, both in the U.S. and worldwide.

Garrett Hardin saw this well over forty years ago when he wrote, "[H]ow do we get the general body politic to accept the truth?"[1] He asked this in 1972, when doing something about growth wasn't as tough, for then there were only *half* as many of us. Since dousing the population bomb came to be near the top of the worldwide to-do list, population has doubled. Since I began talking and writing about overpopulation, population in the U.S. has shot up by half, from two hundred million to over three hundred million. Without the good work done in the 1970s and since, today's population likely would have tripled or worse worldwide.

However, overpopulation being dropped as a worldwide care—being made taboo, as the Optimum Population Trust says, owing to its "sensitivity" for some in our politically correct world—has had outcomes. For one, in Africa's most populous country, Nigeria, the total fertility rate for women sits at 5.49.[2] Forecasts project Nigeria will likely have four hundred forty million people by 2050.[3] Nigeria is not alone among its neighbors just south of the Sahara Desert. All will double their populations in thirty years, and just nineteen percent of women ages fifteen to forty-nine use contraceptives.[4]

Professor Eileen Crist of Virginia Tech has said the best beacons for the harm done by overpopulation sit right under our noses, and she's right. They include wholesale extinction, scalped and plowed wildlands, and catastrophic climate change. However, too many of us don't see—or want to see—that the flood of new mouths makes these crises happen. Others may see it but are afraid on political grounds to say so or they do not have enough like-minded friends to do anything about it.

Then there are those—and I hope that includes you—who do see how population growth (overshoot) and overpopulation drive greenhouse gas pollution, mass extinction, and scalping of wildlands and have the gumption to do something about it. For these bold folk, I offer this to-do list. Some of the things on this list are already being done in one way or another, but it is helpful to bring it all together in one list. Each of us has to choose where we can best work to help freeze and reduce population. All of us who love wild things need to pitch in, whether near to home, nationally, or worldwide.

Conservation To-Do List

Check Out Organizations Run by Conservation Leaders

Start with these two:

1) Apply the Brakes (http://applythebrakes.org)

This organization, formed by long-time leading conservationists, provides an online forum where leaders in the conservation movement present their positions on a comprehensive approach to sustainability. Learning from these experts will help you think out your own stand and make you stronger as you talk about overpopulation. The site also provides you with opportunities to read about ways to halt growth and take action, including contacting your Congressional representatives.

2) The Rewilding Institute Website (www.rewilding.org)

My cohorts and I formed this site to offer information about "the integration of traditional wildlife and wildlands conservation with conservation biology to advance landscape-scale conservation. It provides explanations of key concepts with downloadable documents and links to important papers, essential books, and many groups working on various continental-scale conservation initiatives in North America." A key part of this includes many resources to learn more about overpopulation.

Help Gather Information on How Population Growth Leads to Ecological Wounds

In Chapter 4, I discussed overpopulation and the Seven Ecological Wounds. More knowledge needs to be gathered in this area, such as threatened species and extinction, wildland loss, and the greenhouse threat. Worldwide case studies on how population growth worsens the harm we do to wildlife and wildlands need to be collected. Conservationists, nature writers, and scientists have a landslide of facts and tales of how we are ransacking and slaughtering life on Earth. But we have not carefully linked this killing and harming of wild things to population growth. More needs to be out there that clearly lays out how population growth and overpopulation drive the Seven Ecological Wounds and their outcomes. More rock-hard numbers on the population explosion need to be gathered together.

Help collect this kind of critical information. If you find articles or scientific studies that tie ecological wounds to population growth, send them to: The Rewilding Institute, POB 13768, Albuquerque, NM 87192 or to TRI@rewilding.org.

Speak Out About How Overpopulation Drives Ecological Wounds

More of us need to talk about how the growing Man swarm is the underlying threat to life on Earth. Don't hesitate to write about the causes and problems of population growth and overpopulation in letters to the editor, op-eds, blog comments, and other places in print and online where population and related issues are being discussed.

If you are in college, think about doing your thesis or dissertation on how population growth drives species extinction and other ecological wounds.

If you are a journalist, university professor, in the media, or anyone else with a platform, write and talk about how overpopulation drives conservation problems.

Whenever the opportunity presents itself, use what you have learned in this book, at Apply the Brakes and Rewilding websites to talk about the need to decrease our population.

Organize Speaking Events

Identify conservation leaders at Apply the Brakes website, resource authors on the Rewilding website, and other conservation driven websites. Find those who are in your area, and contact them about giving a talk on overpopulation. If they do not live in your area, ask them who they might know in your area who can speak on the overpopulation issue.

Tell People About This Book

This book is available through Amazon in soft cover and as an e-book. Encourage people to check out the book's page on Amazon, and tell them why they have to buy it. Better yet, tell them why they have to read it and give it to them.

Back Organizations that do Tough Work on Overpopulation

Hail wilderness and wildlife groups that take a strong stand on overpopulation. Send them money, and let them know you are backing them thanks to their work on overpopulation. Drop support to groups that hold weak positions on overpopulation and tell them why you are leaving.

Join Progressives for Immigration Reform

Philip Cafaro and others founded Progressives for Immigration Reform (www.progressivesforimmigrationreform. org) to make the progressive case for lowering immigration. Use their information and arguments to talk to people you know about the need to cut immigration in order to stabilize population in the U.S. Back their work to cap U.S. population growth to protect wild things.

Urge Conservation Groups to Take Strong Stands on Overpopulation and Create Common Ground with Family Planning Advocates and Groups

Conservation organization leaders and board members need to hear from their members and staffers that overpopulation should be acknowledged as the root of ecological wounds. Groups should not drop the work they are already doing, but at least they should talk about overpopulation and the need for freezing. When a group to which you belong starts an activist campaign on sprawl, open space, or other issues, join the campaign—and work to make sure it highlights how population is behind the plight.

In their top-notch paper, "Family Planning and Reproductive Health: The Link to Environmental Preservation," Dr. Joseph Speidel and his associates at the Bixby Center for Reproductive Health at the University of California, San Francisco called for environmentalists and conservationists to work together with family planning advocates.[5] The report shows what better-funded family planning assistance around the world and in the U.S. could do for slowing growth. Give this report to conservation groups, and encourage them to work with family planning advocates such as Dr. Speidel and the Bixby Center.

Adopt and Promote a Strong, Hopeful Vision, Such as Lester Brown's Plan B

The tireless, visionary, human encyclopedia Lester Brown and his Earth Policy Institute have an eye-catching campaign with their Plan B to save Earth (Plan A is doing what we've been doing—the doom-dealing path we are on). The four slices of Plan B include "the stabilization of the world's population at eight billion by 2040."[6] Commit to this vision and spread the word to those you know to get on board with it as well.

Support National Parks

We need to reduce population, but at the same time we need to keep working to keep wildlands and wildlife from being overrun by Man. The Rewilding website has links to more than one hundred conservation groups dedicated to wildland and wildlife protection. My book, *Rewilding North America*, also outlines hopeful visions and what you can do.

Family To-Do List

Have No Biological Children—or at Most One

There are many things you can do to make both your ecological and wilderness footprints smaller. Drive less. Trade in your gas-guzzler for a higher-mileage car or hybrid. Ride a bicycle, walk, or take the bus or subway. Cut back on things and recycle, make your home more energy efficient or make it solar, eat lower on the food chain, and don't eat ocean fish. There's a lot we can do.

However, there is nothing better you can do to lower your footprint than to have no biological children—or at most one. As David Paxson of World Population Balance says, "One child families can save humanity."[7] Having had no children by choice is a good life, Nancy and I can say. And so can millions of other people who have made the same choice. In the last decade or so more people have come out of the woodwork about having made this choice. A growing number of blogs and resource websites provide information and discussion on having no children by choice, such as http://thechildfreelife.com, http://childfreevoices.com, and http://whynokids.com. More books have been published about this life choice than ever before. The book, *The Baby Matrix: Why Freeing Our Minds From Outmoded Thinking About Parenthood & Reproduction Will Create a Better World*, by Laura Carroll, drills deeper from a sociological perspective and challenges the assumptions our society has had about parenthood for generations. Those with no children by choice are demystifying the idea that "the" path to fulfillment in life needs to include parenthood, and are exemplifying the many ways to have a full, rich life without being a mother or father. It can include being a godparent, aunt/uncle or mentor role with children. Nancy and I—we have nieces, nephews, grandnephews, and grandnieces we love.

But—if your soul searching leads you to decide that your life will not be whole without having your own biological children, then have only one. After that, if you want to raise more children, adopt those already here in need of loving homes. If you think your one child needs a sibling, think again. Studies tell us that "onlies" will not automatically be lonely and spoiled just because they don't have siblings. Studies also tell us that the research that originally "concluded" these kinds of things was actually seriously flawed.

If you know you do not want to bring children or any more children into the world, seek permanent birth control now. Get a vasectomy, have a tubal ligation, or check into the non-surgical sterilization procedure called Essure. There will never be a better time.

Encourage and Educate Friends and Loved Ones

When my niece became pregnant with her second child, she told me not to worry: it would be the last one. Like others I know, I told her what more human births means to Earth and wild things. Have the courage to do the same; boldly communicate to your family and friends that we live in an overpopulated world and that the problem can be solved by having one biological child. We need to act as a counterweight to societal messaging that exalts having one's "own" child and promotes going to all lengths, from IVF to egg freezing to try and make it happen.

Cut Your Household's Footprint

As you know by now, Population is the big deal in I=PAT. But we still need to lower our ecological and wilderness footprints by using less energy and buying fewer things. While we must underline that freezing and lowering population has to happen, we also need to curb our consumption, as it too drives ecological wounds.

Political and Economic To-Do List

Set a Goal of Zero Population Growth by the Earliest Doable Date

Set a Population Ceiling for the U.S. that We Will Not Go Beyond

Setting the goals comes first. Making up our minds to stop population growth by a set time at a set number leads to the need to cap immigration. For the sake of a target, I'll call for a population of the United States of no more than 325 million, with zero population growth gained by 2025. It would be better if it could be lower than this. And we should work to lower it after 2025. How about a goal for a U.S. population of no more than two hundred million by 2100? With such goals, we can better figure out what we need to do to reach them. Citizens of other countries also need to set and employ strategies to reach their own population reduction goals.

Call on Your Government to Set a Cap on Population

National commissions should be set up in every country to set what the highest population should be, and Earth lovers need to watchdog them to keep the population cap low. Rosamund McDougall of the Optimum Population Trust writes, "At the end of 2008, Britain became the first country in the EU to set a cap on population growth, with a ministerial pledge not to allow it to grow beyond seventy million." The United Kingdom now has sixty-three million inhabitants and is growing by 500,000 a year thanks to immigration and a too-high birth rate. McDougall warns that the pro-growth policies of British governments "look like a catastrophic environmental error. It is hard to see how the country will be able to sustain seventy million people in 2050." The Optimum Population Trust is calling for "numerically balanced immigration" and "stopping at two children." They believe such a path could cut population to fifty-five million by 2050.[8] The U.S. and other countries need to follow the lead of the Trust.

Call for Long-Term Lowering of World Population to no More than Two Billion

When we get right down to it, freezing world and U.S. population is not nearly enough. J. Kenneth Smail, an anthropology professor at Kenyon College in Ohio, showed that there is truly no choice but to sharply lower the population of Man over the next one hundred to two hundred years. In two articles in European academic journals, Smail lays out a sound, watertight framework to bring the population of Man down to about two billion. His seminal articles are: "Beyond Population Stabilization: The Case for Dramatically Reducing Global Human Numbers" in *Politics and the Life Sciences,* September 1997, and "Confronting a Surfeit of People: Reducing Global Human Numbers to Sustainable Levels" in *Environment, Development and Sustainability,* July 2002. Smail's article in *Politics and the Life Sciences* drew "Roundtable Commentaries" in the same issue from a sweep of scholars, some with their heads in the sand and others backing him with worthwhile thinking and knowledge.[9]

Today, we need to educate people on Smail's framework and make these articles widely available. We need to lay the groundwork for such implementing a population reduction campaign.

Tell Governments and International Agencies to Stop Programs that Foster Births

Write your leaders (president, prime minister, members of congress or parliament) and ask them to take a stand on population reduction. Ask them to support family planning policies that support access to information and services and that will cap immigration. Seek out and talk to representatives and their staff in your city and state about population growth, overpopulation, and immigration.

Call for No Subsidies or Tax Cuts for Two or More Children

Many governments encourage more biological births with subsidies and tax benefits. Work in your country to end such birth boosting. Stand up against policies that encourage reproduction and work against solving overpopulation.

Back Global Family Planning Efforts

Today's health science lets any woman have no more children than she wants. Throughout the world, women say that they want fewer children. Two big hitches are cost and accessibility. Our goal should be to make contraception widely, easily, and freely accessible for every woman and man on Earth. By *freely*, I mean at no cost for those who can't afford it. Back private organizations that offer such help. Call on your government to link all foreign aid to *working* birth control programs. No foreign aid of any kind, including military, should be given to nations that do not offer family planning help to their citizens or that criminalize abortion.

Sao Paulo, Brazil, took steps in 2007 to get birth control to those in need. The city "is offering 'morning after' contraceptive pills at metro stops and ninety percent off contraceptive pills at pharmacies," reports *The Christian Science Monitor*. Men are offered free vasectomies by the Health Ministry, which is also working with teachers to teach sex education and give condoms to students. Since one-in-three pregnancies in Sao Paulo is unwanted, these bold steps will lower unwanted births and sharply cut abortions.[10] Steps like these are needed in countries throughout the world—even in the U.S. and Great Britain.

The third big hitch in family planning is the heartless bullying (and worse) of women by men in much of the world that keeps women from using birth control or makes them afraid to use it. Birth control availability needs to be such that a woman can get it whether her male partner wants it or not.

Family planning and lowering the birth rate can greatly improve health and reduce poverty. However, millions of women in developing countries lack access to contraceptives and voluntary family planning information and services. In 2012, about eighty million women in developing countries had unintended pregnancies. And of those women, at least one in four resorted to an unsafe abortion.[11]

There are organizations working on serious global family planning goals. Take the Bill & Melinda Gates Foundation. Its family planning goal is "to bring access to high-quality contraceptive information, services, and supplies to an additional one hundred twenty million women and girls in the poorest countries by 2020 without coercion or discrimination, with the longer-term goal of universal access to voluntary family planning." Support this organization and others dedicated to global family planning.

Ask other private foundations and health agencies working on world health to put family planning in all their work. The many private groups spending hundreds of millions of dollars a year on childhood diarrhea, malaria, AIDS, tuberculosis, childhood malnutrition, and other health woes in the third world would take more suffering out of the world by far if they made sure that birth control was in the hands of every woman in the world who wants it. Recall what Lyndon Johnson said: "Five dollars invested in population control is worth one hundred dollars invested in economic growth."[12]

Back Organizations that Work to Strengthen Family Planning in Other Countries

In addition to organizations dedicated to family planning and world health, support organizations that do work to support these goals. For example, Population Media Center does amazing work by producing birth control themed soap operas on television in many third-world countries. Check out http://populationmedia.org and support their work.

Back Women's Equality and Education Worldwide

Helping women to raise their standing in benighted lands will do much to bring down birth rates. It is also the right thing to do for the welfare and freedom of women everywhere.

Work Locally to Control Growth

Ask your city council to set an optimal population for your city or town—or run for the council and do it yourself. Even towns that talk about "smart growth" do nothing to think about how big they want to get. By setting an optimal population ceiling, your community has a strong handle on growth.

Back tax, zoning, and transportation policies that will put a damper on growth in your town and region.

Work to help your society shift from an endless-growth economy to a steady-state economy—learn more from the Center for the Advancement of the Steady State Economy at http://steadystate.org.

Call for Capping the Grid in Your Country

Capping the Grid means that a country will not produce or consume more energy than what it is doing now. As more kinds of energy that are greenhouse-friendly come on line, the worse kinds—coal-fired power plants and hydroelectric dams—come down. Learn more about Capping the Grid and campaigns at http://energy-reality.org.

Back Smaller Ecological Footprints, Call out Bad Wilderness Footprints

Lowering births is the key to lowering the ecological and wilderness footprints of Mankind on Earth. At the same time we need to lower how high on the hog we live. Americans, Australians, and Canadians foremost, folks in wealthy lands can lower the *quantity* of their lives without lowering the *quality* of their lives. People in Western European nations and Japan live as well as Americans, Australians, and Canadians, and sometimes better, but with lesser footprints. At the least, the three fat countries need to cut back to consumption levels of Japan and Sweden.

However, some of the ecological footprint standouts such as Japan and Norway sit at the bottom of the barrel for wilderness footprint. Slaughtering great whales is only one of their many sins against wild things at home and worldwide. More of us need to harp on how Japan, Norway, and other countries with middling ecological footprints but dreadful wilderness footprints act as hypocrites and even international outlaws. We need to find more ways to shame them into stopping whale murdering, overfishing, and other crimes against wild things.

Ask Your Members of Congress to Help Cap Immigration

If you don't already, go to local meetings with your members of Congress. Talk with them about what you have learned about the links between conservation, family planning, and immigration. Tell them why now is the time to return to the 1989 Sierra Club policy—why immigration policies need to be driven by population stabilization goals more than anything else.

Ask that they co-sponsor bills that would cut immigration into the U.S. as well as bills that would raise funding for family planning here and around the world. Ask them to back a legislative ban on all immigration from countries that do not allow legal abortions or that hinder family planning. Insist that they do not back amnesty for those here unlawfully.

Get Your State to Mandate the Use of E-Verify by All Employers

Ask your governor, state representative, and state senator to introduce and sponsor a bill that mandates use of E-verify by all employers in your state to make sure all applicants are in the U.S. lawfully and eligible for employment. Getting your state to require its use by all employers might do more than anything else to halt unlawful immigration.

There's a lot we can do. If we do these things, we will shrink the Man swarm for the sake of the Earth and us all.

ENDNOTES

Introduction

1. Steven LeBlanc with Katherine Register, *Constant Battles: The Myth of the Peaceful, Noble Savage* (St. Martin's Press, New York, 2003), 30.

Chapter 1: Man's Population Explosion

1. Dave Foreman, *Rewilding North America: A Vision for Conservation in the Twenty-first Century* (Island Press, Washington, DC, 2004). In Part A of *Rewilding North America* I look in depth at extinction.

2. Kind has long been used in English, even by Darwin, to mean species.

3. *Hominin* is a rather new term human paleontologists use for species in the kinship group of Man, not that of other apes.

4. Nicholas Wade, *Before the Dawn: Recovering the Lost History of Our Ancestors* (The Penguin Press, New York, 2006), 52.

5. Man found Iceland, New Zealand, Madagascar, and Hawaii only in the last two thousand years or less.

6. Dave Foreman, *Rewilding North America*. Paul Martin and Richard Klein, eds., *Quaternary Extinctions: A Prehistoric Revolution* (University of Arizona Press, Tucson, 1984).

7. Richard Cincotta, ecologist and senior researcher, Population Action International, 2002.

8. J. R. McNeill and William McNeill, *The Human Web: A Bird's-Eye View of World History* (W. W. Norton & Company, New York, 2003), 221. Sumer, between the Tigris and Euphrates rivers, is the first known city.

9. Ibid.

10. Warren Hern, "How Many Times Has the Human Population Doubled? Comparisons with Cancer," *Population and Environment: A Journal of Interdisciplinary Studies,* Vol. 21, Number 1, September 1999, 59-80. (Population doubling time is the number of years it takes a population to double.)

11. Warren Hern, "Has The Human Species Become A Cancer On The Planet? A Theoretical View Of Population Growth As A Sign Of Pathology," *Current World Leaders: Biography & News/Speeches & Reports Issue,* Vol. 36, No. 6, December 1993.

12. Garrett Hardin, *Living Within Limits: Ecology, Economics, and Population Taboos* (Oxford University Press, New York, 1993), 11-12.

13. Anne Ehrlich, "Implications of Population Pressure on Agriculture and Ecosystems," *Advances in Botanical Research*, Vol. 21, 1995, 84.

14. J. Kenneth Smail, "Confronting A Surfeit of People: Reducing Global Human Numbers To Sustainable Levels," *Environment, Development and Sustainability* 4, July 2002, Kluwer Academic Publishers, the Netherlands, 24.

15. Smail, "Confronting A Surfeit Of People," 24.

16. J. Joseph Speidel, MD, Cover Letter for "Family Planning and Reproductive Health: The Link to Environmental Preservation," January 18, 2008.

Chapter 2: The Great Shortsightedness

1. Roy Beck and Leon Kolankiewicz, "The Environmental Movement's Retreat from Advocating U.S. Population Stabilization (1970-1998): A First Draft of History," *Journal Of Policy History,* Vol. 12, No. 1, 2000, 123. An abridgement was reprinted in *Wild Earth,* Summer 2001, 66-67.

2. Paul Ehrlich and Anne Ehrlich, *Population Resources Environment: Issues In Human Ecology* (W. H. Freeman and Company, San Francisco, 1970).

3. Elisabeth Rosenthal, "An Amazon Culture Withers as Food Dries Up," *New York Times,* July 25, 2009.

4. Reuters, "Water Crisis Uproots Syrian Farmers," *New York Times,* July 26, 2009.

5. Garrett Hardin, "We Live on a Spaceship," *Bulletin of the Atomic Scientists,* XXIII (1972), 23-25, reprinted in Roderick Frazier Nash, ed., *American Environmentalism: Readings In Conservation History* Third Edition (McGraw-Hill, New York, 1990), 238.

6. George Sessions, "Political Correctness, Ecological Realities and the Future of the Ecology Movement," *The Trumpeter,* Fall 1995, 191.

7. Eileen Crist, "Limits-to-Growth and the Biodiversity Crisis," *Wild Earth*, Spring 2003, 63.

8. Ibid.

9. Crist, "Limits-to-Growth," 64.

10. Crist, "Limits-to-Growth," 65.

11. *The Guardian*, San Francisco, December 7, 2005.

12. Reed F. Noss, Edward T. LaRoe, and J. Michael Scott, *Endangered Ecosystems of the United States: A Preliminary Assessment of Loss and Degradation,* Biological Report 28 (National Biological Service, U.S. Department of the Interior, Washington, D.C., February 1995); Reed F. Noss and Robert L. Peters, *Endangered Ecosystems: A Status Report on America's Vanishing Habitat and Wildlife* (Defenders of Wildlife, Washington, D.C., December 1995).

Chapter 3: Redefining Carrying Capacity

1. William Catton Jr., *Overshoot: The Ecological Basis of Revolutionary Change* (University of Illinois Press, Urbana, 1982), 216-217.

2. Jared Diamond, *The Third Chimpanzee: The Evolution and Future of the Human Animal* (HarperCollins, New York, 1992), 324-325.

3. Eileen Crist, letter to author, 2010.

4. Catton, *Overshoot,* 126.

5. Catton, *Overshoot,* 126-7.

6. Catton, *Overshoot*, 24.

7. William McNeill, *Plagues and Peoples*, (Anchor Press/Doubleday, New York, 1976). In this book, McNeill upends world history to show how greatly diseases have driven the saga of world civilization.

8. Dave Foreman, *Rewilding North America*, (Island Press, Washington, D.C., 2004). These other hominin species were *Homo neanderthalensis, Homo erectus, and Homo florensis,* and maybe others.

9. Catton, *Overshoot,* 26-28.

10. Catton, *Overshoot,* 28-30. See also J. R. McNeill and William McNeill, *The Human Web: A Bird's-Eye View of World History,* (W.W. Norton & Company, New York, 2003)

11. Catton, *Overshoot,* 158-159.

12. Stuart Pimm, *The World According to Pimm: A Scientist Audits the Earth*, (McGraw-Hill, New York, 2001), 10.

13. Paul Ehrlich and Anne Ehrlich, *The Population Explosion*, (Simon and Schuster, New York, 1990), 36-37. (163).

14. Pimm, *The World According to Pimm.* See also Foreman, Rewilding North America, 56-59.

15. Catton, *Overshoot,* 172-173.

16. Reg Morrison, *The Spirit in the Gene: Humanity's Proud Illusion and the Laws of Nature*, (Cornell University Press, Ithaca, New York, 1999).

Chapter 4: How the Man Swarm Eats the Earth

1. E. O. Wilson, "Acting now to save life on Earth," *Seattle Post-Intelligencer,* April 22, 2007. Adapted from his book, *The Creation.*

2. "Owning Up to Overpopulation," *Endangered Earth,* Fall 2009, Center for Biological Diversity.

3. Lester Brown, "Could Food Shortages Bring Down Civilization?" *Scientific American,* April 22, 2009.

4. Lester Brown, "Food Shortages." See also Lester Brown, *Plan B 3.0: Mobilizing to Save Civilization* (W.W. Norton & Co., New York, 2008); available from www.earthpolicy.org/Books/PB3/index.htm.

5. Philip Cafaro and Winthrop Staples, "The Environmental Argument for Reducing Immigration to the United States," *Backgrounder,* Center for Immigration Studies, June 2009, 3.

6. *The Guardian,* San Francisco, December 7, 2005.

7. Coomi Kapoor, "Indian tigers' days numbered," India Diary, *The Star,* March 3, 2008.

8. Norman Myers, "Biodiversity: What's At Stake," *Pop!ulation Press,* Population Coalition, Redlands, CA, September/October 2002, 7.

9. Claudine LoMonaco, "Migrants intrude; scarce pronghorn die," *Tucson Citizen,* July 1, 2005.

10. See my book, *Rewilding North America* for more on this much-needed job by flesh-eating animals.

11. Daniel McKinley, "Preface Two," in Paul Shepard and Daniel McKinley, editors, *Environ/Mental: Essays on the Planet as Home* (Houghton Mifflin Co., Boston, 1971), ix.

12. Paul Ehrlich and John Holdren, "Population and Panaceas A Technological Perspective," *BioScience* Vol. 19, (December, 1969), 1065-1071, reprinted in *Environ/Mental,* 265.

13. John Holdren and Paul Ehrlich, "Impact of Population Growth," Science Vol. 171 (1974), 1212-17.

14. Paul Ehrlich and Anne Ehrlich, *The Population Explosion* (Simon and Schuster, New York, 1990), 58.

15. John Cleland, Stan Bernstein, Alex Ezeh, Anibal Faundes, Anna Glasier, and Jolene Innis, "Family planning: the unfinished agenda," *The Lancet,* November 18, 2006.

16. A Population-Based Climate Strategy—An Optimum Population Trust Briefing, May 2007, http://populationmatters.org/documents/climate_strategy.pdf, accessed March 2014.

17. News Release "Combat Climate Change with Fewer Babies— OPT Report," Optimum Population Trust, May 7, 2007, http://www. populationmatters.org/2007/press/combat-climate-change-babies-opt-report/, accessed March 2014.

18. A Population-Based Climate Strategy—An Optimum Population Trust Briefing.

19. Elisabeth Rosenthal, "Third-World Stove Soot Is Target in Climate Fight," *New York Times,* April 16, 2009.

20. Ibid.

21. Ibid.

22. Ibid.

23. Cafaro and Staples, "Environmental Arguments," 5.

24. This table shows population for selected countries in 1940-1950, today, and projected for 2050. It also shows the percentage of the 2010 population under fifteen years of age and a sampling of the species endangered by population growth. Sources: population 1940-1950: The International Standard Atlas of the World (Book Production Industries, Chicago, 1949) from "most authoritative estimates available"; population 2010 and 2050: The World Almanac 2011 (World Almanac Books, New York, 2010) from Population Division, U.S. Census Bureau; and The World Factbook, Central Intelligence Agency. Wildlife presence is drawn from various sources, including Dr. David Macdonald, ed., The Encyclopedia of Mammals (Facts on File, New York, 1985). Note: The first version of this table was based on The World Almanac 2008, which drew on the same sources but three years earlier. Population figures for 2010 and especially forecasts for 2050 had to be broadly revised, some higher and some lower. This shows that population figures for third-world countries are far from exact. For example the 2050 forecast for Ethiopia here is 278.3 million; the 2008 forecast was 144.7 million, an outlandish difference of 130 million. On the other hand, the 2050 forecast here for Nigeria is 264.3 million; the 2008 forecast was 356.5 million, about a 90 million difference.

Chapter 5: The Cornucopian Mindset

1. Norman Myers and Julian Simon, *Scarcity or Abundance: A Debate on the Environment* (W. W. Norton, New York, 1994), 65.

2. Sandy Irvine, "The Great Denial: Puncturing Pro-natalist Myths," *Wild Earth*, Winter 1997/98, 8.

3. See Garrett Hardin, *Living Within Limits: Ecology, Economics, and Population Taboos* (Oxford University Press, New York, 1993), 5.

4. Irvine, "The Great Denial," 14.

5. Marvin Harris, *Cannibals and Kings* (Vintage Books, New York, 1991), 271. Communist International, or the Comintern, was a board of directors of sorts for the international Communist movement.

6. David Ehrenfeld, *The Arrogance of Humanism* (Oxford University Press, New York, 1981), 16-17.

7. Paul S. Sutter, Driven *Wild: How the Fight Against Automobiles Launched the Modern Wilderness Movement*, (University of Washington Press, Seattle, 2002).

8. Robert Merry, *Sands of Empire: Missionary Zeal, American Foreign Policy, and the Hazards of Global Ambition* (Simon & Schuster, New York, 2005), 7.

9. Eugene Linden, *The Future In Plain Sight: Nine Clues To The Coming Instability* (Simon & Schuster, New York, 1998), 140.

10. I further delve into the Myth of Superabundance in *Taming the Wilderness and The Nature Haters*.

11. William Catton Jr., *Overshoot: The Ecological Basis of Revolutionary Change* (University of Illinois Press, Urbana, 1982), xii.

12. Henry Luce, "Endless Frontiers," *Time*, July 30, 1951; quoted in Jon M. Cosco, *Echo Park: Struggle for Preservation* (Johnson Books, Boulder, Co, 1995).

13. Rose DeWolf, "Yesterday's Tomorrow," *New York Times Magazine*, December 24, 1995.

14. Edward Deevey, Jr., "The Human Population," *Scientific American* 203(3), September 1960, 195-204; reprinted in Paul Shepard and Daniel McKinley, editors, *The Subversive Science* (Houghton Mifflin, Boston, 1969), 52.

15. *Time*, January 6, 1967.

16. Herman Kahn and Anthony Wiener, *The Year 2000* (Macmillan, New York, 1967), quoted in Ehrenfeld, *Arrogance of Humanism*, 45.

17. Robert Solow, "The economics of resources or the resources of economics," *American Economics Review,* 64, 1974, 1-14, quoted in William E. Rees and Mathis Wackernagel, "Ecological Footprints And Appropriated Carrying Capacity: Measuring The Natural Capital Requirements Of The Human Economy," *Focus,* Vol. 6, No. 1, 1996, Carrying Capacity Network, 47.

18. Hardin, *Living Within Limits*, 44-45.

19. Paul Ehrlich, "An Ecologist Standing Up Among Seated Social Scientists," *CoEvolution Quarterly* 31 (1981), 28, quoted in Hardin, *Living Within Limits,* 193.

20. Hardin, *Living Within Limits*, 191.

21. U.S. National Research Council, Population Growth and Economic Development: Policy Questions (National Academy Press, Washington, D.C., 1986), 15-16.

22. Gregg Easterbrook, "Living Large; There'll soon be 300 million of us. But don't worry, there's plenty of room." *Los Angeles Times,* October 8, 2006.

23. Myers and Simon, *Scarcity or Abundance*, 65.

24. Paul Ehrlich and Anne Ehrlich, *Betrayal of Science and Reason: How Anti-Environmental Rhetoric Threatens Our Future* (Island Press, Washington, D.C., 1996), 66. In case you don't want to do the math yourself, the Ehrlichs do it on page 264.

25. Ibid.

26. Albert A. Bartlett, "The Exponential Function, XI: The New Flat Earth Society," *Focus,* Carrying Capacity Network, Vol. 7, No. 1, 1997, 34-36.

27. Ibid.

28. Irvine, "The Great Denial," 12.

29. Hardin, *Living Within Limits*, 307.

30. Garrett Hardin, "An Ecolate View of the Human Predicament," http://www.garretthardinsociety.org/articles/art_ecolate_view_human_predicament.html, accessed March 2014.

31. Steven LeBlanc with Katherine Register, *Constant Battles: The Myth of the Peaceful, Noble Savage* (St. Martin's Press, NY, 2003), 54.

Chapter 6: Birth Dearth Follies

1. Phillip Longman, "The Global Baby Bust," *Foreign Affairs,* May/June 2004.

2. Chris Mooney, *The Republican War on Science* (Basic Books, New York, 2005). Mooney does a tip-top job of showing how the right-wing lynching of science and scientists from the health threat of tobacco to global warming is a clever public-relations game for big business.

3. Steve Camarota, "100 million More—Projecting the Impact of Immigration on the U.S. Population, 2007-2060," http://ww.cis.org/articles/2007/back707.html.

Chapter 7: Was Paul Ehrlich Really Wrong?

1. Marvin Harris, *Our Kind* (Harper & Row, New York, 1989), 497.

2. Paul Ehrlich and Anne Ehrlich, *The Population Bomb* (Sierra Club-Ballantine Books, New York, 1968).

3. Lester Brown, "Could Food Shortages Bring Down Civilization? *Scientific American,* April 22, 2009.

4. Paul Ehrlich and Anne Ehrlich, *Betrayal of Science and Reason: How Anti-Environmental Rhetoric Threatens Our Future* (Island Press, Washington, DC, 1996), 71-76.

5. Clive Ponting, *A Green History of The World* (St. Martin's Press, New York, 1991), 252.

6. Lester Brown, *Outgrowing the Earth* (W.W. Norton, New York, 2004).

7. Harris, *Our Kind*, 497-498.

8. Ibid.

9. Paul Sabin, *The Bet: Paul Ehrlich, Julian Simon, and Our Gamble over Earth's Future* (Yale University Press, Connecticut, 2013), 4.

10. Julian Simon, "Earth's Doomsayers are Wrong," *San Francisco Chronicle,* May 12, 1995.

11. Paul Ehrlich and Stephen Schneider, "Bets and 'Ecofantasies,'" *Environmental Awareness*, Vol. 18, No. 2, 1995, 47-50.

12. Ehrlich and Ehrlich, *Betrayal of Science and Reason,* 100-104.

Chapter 8: A History of Thinking about Man's Limits

1. Garrett Hardin, *Living Within Limits: Ecology, Economics, and Population Taboos* (Oxford University Press, New York, 1993), 17.

2. Quoted in H. C. Darby, "The Clearing of the Woodland in Europe," in William L. Thomas Jr., ed., *Man's Role In Changing The Face Of The Earth* (University of Chicago Press, 1956), 185.

3. Clarence Glacken, "Changing Ideas of the Habitable World," in *Man's Role In Changing The Face Of The Earth*, (University of Chicago Press, 1956), 70-92.

4. Paul Sears, *Deserts on the March* (University of Oklahoma Press, Norman, 1980 (1935). Sears retired to northern New Mexico. I was thrilled in 1972 when he wrote me to back my work against building Cochiti Dam on the Rio Grande.

5. Sears, *Deserts on the March*, vi.

6. Carl Sauer, "Theme of Plant and Animal Destruction in Economic History," *Journal of Farm Economics* 20 (1938), 765-775, reprinted in Paul Shepard and Daniel McKinley, editors, *Environ/Mental: Essays on the Planet as Home* (Houghton Mifflin, Boston, 1971), 54.

7. W. C. Lowdermilk, *Conquest of the Land Through 7,000 Years,* Agriculture Information Bulletin No. 99, U.S. Dept. of Agriculture, Soil Conservation Service, August 1953. The Department of Agriculture was still handing out copies of Lowdermilk's report in the early 1970s when I got my copy. Soil conservation was still a crusade then. We don't seem to think much about it today. We will pay for that.

8. Fairfield Osborn, *Our Plundered Planet* (Little, Brown and Company, Boston, 1948).

9. William Vogt, *Road to Survival* (William Sloane Associates, New York, 1948), 284. Excerpted as "The Global Perspective" in Roderick Frazier Nash, ed., *American Environmentalism: Readings in Conservation History* Third Edition (McGraw-Hill, New York, 1990), 166. Vogt strongly backed the campaign against the Sagebrush Rebellion's attempt to steal the public lands in the late 1970s (I was a player in this campaign).

10. Luna Leopold, ed., *Round River: From the Journals of Aldo Leopold* (Oxford University Press, New York, 1953), 165.

11. Paul Shepard and Daniel McKinley, editors, *The Subversive Science: Essays Toward an Ecology of Man* (Houghton Mifflin, Boston, 1969).

12. Vernon Gill Carter and Tom Dale, *Topsoil and Civilization* Revised Edition (University of Oklahoma Press, Norman, 1974), 20.

13. William Leroy Thomas, *Man's Role in Changing the Face of the Earth,* (University of Chicago Press, 1956). I have read this mighty work more than once and find it still loaded with sharp insights and sorely needed information. In some academic fields, work done decades ago has not been bettered. *Man's Role* is proof of that.

14. Luna Leopold was a great hydrologist and died in early 2006.

15. Thomas, *Man's Role,* 1115.

16. Thomas, *Man's Role,* 1117.

17. Richard Heinberg, *The Party's Over: Oil, War and the Fate of Industrial Societies* (New Society Publishers, Gabriola Island, British Columbia, Canada, 2003), 88.

18. David Ehrenfeld, *The Arrogance of Humanism* (Oxford University Press, NY, 1978), 115.

19. David Brower, "Foreword" in Paul Ehrlich, *The Population Bomb* (Ballantine Books/Sierra Club, New York, 1968).

20. Paul Ehrlich, *The Population Bomb* (Ballantine Books/Sierra Club, New York, 1968), 34.

21. Donella Meadows, Dennis Meadows, Jorgen Randers, and William Behrens, *The Limits to Growth* (Universe Books, New York, 1972), 23.

22. Donella Meadows, Dennis Meadows, and Jorgen Randers, *Beyond the Limits: Confronting Global Collapse, Envisioning a Sustainable Future* (Chelsea Green Publishing Company, Post Mills, VT, 1992); Donella Meadows, Jorgen Randers, and Dennis Meadows, *Limits to Growth: The 30-Year Update* (Chelsea Green Publishing Company, White River Junction, VT, 2004).

23. Dave Foreman, *Rewilding North America* (Island Press, Washington, DC, 2004), 20.

24. Keith Murray, Berkeley Ecology Center, "Suggestions Toward an Ecological Platform" in Garrett de Bell, Editor, *The Environmental Handbook* (Ballantine/Friends of the Earth, New York, 1970), 317-324.

25. Ehrlich and Ehrlich, *The Population Explosion*, (Simon and Schuster, New York, 1990); Garrett Hardin, *Living Within Limits: Ecology, Economics, and Population Taboos* (Oxford University Press, New York, 1993), and *The Ostrich Factor: Our Population Myopia* (Oxford University Press, New York, 1999).

26. William Catton, Jr., *Overshoot: The Ecological Basis of Revolutionary Change* (University of Illinois Press, Urbana and Chicago, 1982).

27. Reg Morrison, *The Spirit in the Gene: Humanity's Proud Illusion and the Laws of Nature* (Cornell University Press, Ithaca, New York, 1999).

28 E.O.Wilson, back cover blurb, Morrison, *The Spirit in the Gene.*

29. Morrison, *The Spirit in the Gene*, xi.

30. William McNeill, *Plagues and Peoples* (Anchor Press/Doubleday, New York, 1976).

31. J. R. McNeill and William McNeill, *The Human Web: A Bird's-Eye View of World History* (W.W. Norton & Company, New York, 2003), 210-211.

32. Richard Heinberg, *The Party's Over: Oil, War and the Fate of Industrial Societies* (New Society Publishers, Gabriola Island, British Columbia, Canada, 2003), 187.

33. Michael T. Klare, *Resource Wars: The New Landscape of Global Conflict* (Henry Holt and Company, New York, 2002), 15.

34. Klare, *Resource Wars*, 25.

35. Samuel Huntington, *The Clash of Civilizations and the Remaking of World Order* (Simon & Schuster, New York, 1996), 116.

36. Lester Brown, *Outgrowing The Earth: The Food Security Challenge In An Age Of Falling Water Tables And Rising Temperatures* (W.W. Norton & Company, New York, 2004).

Chapter 9: The Great Backtrack

1. Martin Luther King, Jr., Speech given after getting Margaret Sanger Award in Human Rights, 1966. Quoted in Paul Ehrlich and Anne Ehrlich, *Population Resources Environment: Issues in Human Ecology* (W. H. Freeman and Company, San Francisco, 1970), 211.

2. "U.S. Population on Track to 300 Million," *New York Times,* October 14, 2006.

3. John Tierney, "The Kids Are All Right," *New York Times,* October 14, 2006.

4. David Nicholson-Lord, "Whatever happened to the teeming millions?" http://www.forumforthefuture.org/greenfutures/articles/what ever-happened-teeming-millions, accessed May 2014.

5. Samuel Hays, *Beauty, Health, and Permanence: Environmental Politics in the United States, 1955-1985* (Cambridge University Press, New York, 1987), 224.

6. Quoted in Ehrlich and Ehrlich, *Population Resources Environment*, 259, 295.

7. Hays, *Beauty, Health, and Permanence*, 224.

8. Roy Beck and Leon Kolankiewicz, "The Environmental Movement's Retreat from Advocating U.S. Population Stabilization (1970-1998): A First Draft of History," https://www.numbersusa.com/sites/default/files/public/from_drupal5/pdf/Retreat2.pdf, accessed May 2014, and Leon Kolankiewicz and Roy Beck, "Forsaking Fundamentals: The Environmental Establishment Abandons U.S. Population Stabilization," Center for Immigration Studies, April 2001, http://www.cis.org/sites/cis.org/files/articles/2001/forsaking/forsaking.pdf, accessed May 2014.

9. William Ryerson, "Political Correctness and the Population Problem," *Wild Earth*, Winter 1998/99, 100-103.

10. Kolankiewicz and Beck, "Forsaking Fundamentals," 3-4.

11. Ryerson, "Political Correctness."

12. Kolankiewicz and Beck, "Forsaking Fundamentals," 12.

13. Stephanie Mills, *Whatever Happened To Ecology?* (Sierra Club Books, San Francisco, 1989), 51.

14. Ryerson, "Political Correctness," 101.

15. Kolankiewicz and Beck, "Forsaking Fundamentals," 16.

16. Quoted in Donald VanDeVeer and Christine Pierce, editors, *The Environmental Ethics and Policy Book: Philosophy, Ecology, Economics* (Wadsworth Publishing Company, Belmont, California, 1994), 370.

17. Theodore J. Lowi, *The End of The Republican Era* (University of Oklahoma Press, Norman, 1995).

18. Ryerson, "Political Correctness," 102. The United Nations put on an international population conference in 1974 and every ten years thereafter. Each one further watered down the need to stabilize population.

19. Kolankiewicz and Beck, "Forsaking Fundamentals," 18-19.

20. Frances Kissling, "Ban on Contraceptives Antiquated, Dangerous," *Baltimore Sun*, November 14, 2006.

21. John Cleland, Stan Bernstein, Alex Ezeh, Anibal Faundes, Anna Glasier, and Jolene Innis, "Family planning: the unfinished agenda," *The Lancet,* November 18, 2006.

22. Kolankiewicz and Beck, "Forsaking Fundamentals," 21.

23. Somini Sengupta, "As Indian Growths Soars, Child Hunger Persists," *New York Times,* March 13, 2009.

24. Kolankiewicz and Beck, "Forsaking Fundamentals," 28.

25. Richard D. Lamm, "The real bind is too many people everywhere," *High Country News,* September 5, 1994.

26. Philip Cafaro and Winthrop Staples, "The Environmental Argument for Reducing Immigration to the United States," *Backgrounder,* Center for Immigration Studies, June 2009, 3.

27. Sierra Club Population Report, Spring 1989.

28. David Ehrenfeld, *The Arrogance of Humanism* (Oxford University Press, NY, 1978), 235.

29. Eugene Linden, *The Future In Plain Sight: Nine Clues To The Coming Instability* (Simon & Schuster, New York, 1998), 27.

Chapter 10: Population or Affluence— or Technology?

1. Kate Galbraith, "Having Children Brings High Carbon Impact," *New York Times,* August 7, 2009.

2. Steven LeBlanc with Katherine Register, *Constant Battles: The Myth of the Peaceful, Noble Savage* (St. Martin's Press, New York, 2003).

3. Niles Eldredge, "Cretaceous Meteor Showers, the Human Ecological 'Niche,' and the Sixth Extinction," in Ross D. E. MacPhee, editor, *Extinctions in Near Time: Causes, Contexts, and Consequences* (Kluwer Academic/Plenum Publishers, New York, 1999), 13.

4. Leon Kolankiewicz, "From Big to Bigger: How Mass Immigration and Population Growth Have Exacerbated America's Ecological Footprint," Policy Brief # 10-1, March 2010, Progressives for Immigration Reform, 1.

5. Philip Cafaro and Winthrop Staples, "The Environmental Argument for Reducing Immigration to the United States," *Backgrounder,* Center for Immigration Studies, June 2009, 6-7.

6. Cafaro and Staples, "Environmental Argument," 7.

7. Leon Kolankiewicz and Roy Beck, Weighing Sprawl Factors in Large U.S. Cities, NumbersUSA, March 19, 2001, https://www.numbersusa. com/content/files/pdf/LargeCity%20Sprawl.pdf, accessed May 2014.

8. Jeff Dardozzi, "The Specter of Jevons' Paradox," *Synthesis/Regeneration* 47, Fall 2008.

9. John Fleck, "Energy Savings? No, More Light," *Albuquerque Journal,* September 21, 2010.

10. Galbraith, "Having Children Brings High Carbon Impact."

11. Paul Murtaugh and Michael Schlax, "Reproduction and the carbon legacies of individuals," *Global Environmental Change* 19 (2009), 14-20.

12. Media Release, "Family planning: A major environmental emphasis," Oregon State University, July 31, 2009.

Chapter 11: The Thorny Issue of Immigration

1. Philip Martin, "Trends in Migration to the U.S.," *Population Reference Bureau,* June 2, 2014.

2. Gretchen Livingston and D'Vera Cohn, "U.S. Birth Rate Falls to a Record Low; Decline Is Greatest Among Immigrants," Pew Social and Demographic Trends, November 29, 2012, http://www. pewsocialtrends.org/2012/11/29/u-s-birth-rate-falls-to-a-record-low-decline-is-greatest-among-immigrants/, accessed April 2014.

3. Rakesh Kochhar, "10 Projections for the Global Population in 2050," Pew Research FactTank, February 3, 2014, http://www.pewresearch. org/fact-tank/2014/02/03/10-projections-for-the-global-population-in-2050/, accessed April 2014.

4. U.S. Census Bureau, "U.S. Census Bureau Projections Show a Slower Growing, Older, More Diverse Nation a Half Century from Now," December 12, 2012, http://www.census.gov/newsroom/releases/archives/population/cb12-243.html, accessed April 2014.

5. Jennifer M. Ortman and Christine E. Guarneri, "United States Population Projections: 2000 to 2050," U.S. Census Bureau, https://www.census.gov/population/projections/files/analytical-document09.pdf, accessed April 2014.

6. Cafaro and Staples, "The Environmental Argument for Reducing Immigration to the United States," *Backgrounder,* Center for Immigration Studies, June 2009, 7.

7. Cafaro and Staples, "Environmental Argument."

8. Ibid.

9. The Wilderness Society Population Policy, The Wilderness Society, Washington, D.C., February 22, 1996.

10. Cafaro and Staples, "Environmental Argument."

11. Roy Germano, Ph.D., "How many immigrants live in the United States and where do they come from?" May 5, 2012, http://roygermano.com/2012/05/05/how-many-immigrants-live-in-the-united-states-and-where-do-they-come-from/, accessed April 2014.

12. Countries with sea coasts have "exclusive economic zones" stretching out two hundred miles from the coast where they have the rights to fishing, oil and gas drilling, seabed mining, and so on.

13. The World Bank, "Fertility rate, total (births per woman)," http://data.worldbank.org/indicator/SP.DYN.TFRT.IN, accessed April 2014.

14. Stephan Dinan, "Americans want legal immigration cut in half, poll finds," February 21, 2014, http://www.washingtontimes.com/news/2014/feb/21/poll-americans-want-legal-immigration-cut-half/?page=all, accessed April 2014.

15. Center for Immigration Studies, "Minority Advocates, Constituents Differ on Immigration," Washington, DC, February 25, 2010.

Chapter 12: Steps to Capping Immigration to the United States

1. Ruben Navarrette, Jr., "Understand, Don't Demonize, Illegal Immigrants," *Albuquerque Journal,* March 3, 2010.

2. Philip Martin, "Trends in Migration to the U.S.," *Population Reference Bureau*, June 2, 2014.

3. Julia Preston, "Mexican Data Shows Migration to U.S. in Decline," *New York Times*, May 15, 2009.

4. Stephan Dinan, "Americans want legal immigration cut in half, poll finds," February 21, 2014, http://www.washingtontimes.com/news/2014/feb/21/poll-americans-want-legal-immigration-cut-half/?page=all, accessed April 2014.

5. Brian Segee and Jenny Neeley, "On The Line: The Impacts of Immigration Policy on Wildlife and Habitat in the Arizona Borderlands," (Defenders of Wildlife, Washington, D.C., 2006).

6. Segee and Neeley, "On The Line," 37.

7. Peter Goodman, "In Mexico, 'People Do Really Want to Stay,' Chicken Farmers Fear U.S. Exports Will Send More Workers North for Jobs," *Washington Post,* January 7, 2007.

8. Sara Miller Llana, "For Mexicans Seeking to Cross the US Border, It's not Just About Jobs Anymore," *Christian Science Monitor,* September 27, 2009.

9. Philip Cafaro and Winthrop Staples, "The Environmental Argument for Reducing Immigration to the United States," *Backgrounder,* Center for Immigration Studies, June 2009, 15.

10. Jesse McKinley, "In California Forests, Marijuana Growers Thrive," *New York Times,* August 22, 2009.

Chapter 13: What We Can Do

1. Garrett Hardin, "We Live on a Spaceship," *Bulletin of the Atomic Scientists,* XXIII (1972), 23-25, reprinted in Roderick Frazier Nash, ed., *American Environmentalism: Readings In Conservation History* Third Edition (McGraw-Hill, New York, 1990), 238.

2. Total Fertility Rate, Nigeria, https://www.google.com/search?q=climes&rlz=1C1SKPC_enUS449&oq=climes&aqs=chrome.0.57j0j5j0.1769j0&sourceid=chrome&ie=UTF-8#q=total+fertility+rate+nigeria, access May 2014.

3. Y Rakesh Kochhar, "10 Projections for the Global Population for 2050," Pew Research Center, February 3, 2014, http://www.pewresearch.org/fact-tank/2014/02/03/10-projections-for-the-global-population-in-2050/, accessed May 2014.

4. Wikimedia Commons, "Contraceptive Prevalence by Region of Africa," Wikipedia, http://en.wikipedia.org/wiki/File:Contraceptive_Prevelance_by_Region_of_Africa.jpg, accessed May 2014.

5. Dr. Joseph Speidel, et al., "Family Planning and Reproductive Health: The Link to Environmental Preservation," Bixby Center for Reproductive Health Research and Policy, University of California San Francisco, 2007.

6. Lester Brown, "Could Food Shortages Bring Down Civilization?" *Scientific American,* April 22, 2009.

7. Dave Paxson, "Balanced View," World Population Balance newsletter, Spring 2014, 2.

8. Rosamund McDougall, "Defusing the population time bomb," *The National,* May 8, 2009.

9. J. Kenneth Smail, "Beyond Population Stabilization: The Case for Dramatically Reducing Global Human Numbers," *Politics and the Life Sciences,* Vol. 16, No. 2, September 1997, Beech Tree Publishing, Surrey, UK, 183-192; and "Confronting a Surfeit of People: Reducing Global Human Numbers to Sustainable Levels," *Environment, Development and Sustainability,* 4, July 2002, Kluwer, the Netherlands, 21-50.

10. Andrew Downie, "Brazil Doles Out 'Morning After' Pills," *The Christian Science Monitor,* November 20, 2007.

11. The Bill and Melinda Gates Foundation Family Planning Strategic Overview, http://www.gatesfoundation.org/What-We-Do/Global-Development/Family-Planning, accessed May 2014.

12. Quoted in Paul Ehrlich and Anne Ehrlich, *Population Resources Environment: Issues in Human Ecology* (W. H. Freeman and Company, San Francisco, 1970), 259, 295.

ACKNOWLEDGMENTS

For the first edition of *Man Swarm*, I thanked a small swarm of folks who had helped with the book and my understanding of overpopulation, population growth, and the dreaded consequences. I won't repeat it here; instead I will acknowledge those who helped with this second edition.

I must thank David Paxson and Laura Carroll, who approached me with the idea to do a revised edition that would be more appealing and accessible to younger folks—who, after all, are the ones who have the solution to overpopulation and population growth in their hands (well, truly in other parts of their anatomy). I first wrote *Man Swarm* as a call to the conservation fellowship to again make overpopulation a first rank priority—that if we didn't deal with the exploding Man swarm, all our work to save wild things would come to naught. David and Laura had the vision to see that *Man Swarm* could also speak to another audience—one younger, less conservation-driven, and maybe less grounded in biology. I thank them not only for that vision and idea, but also for having the drive to make this new edition happen.

When David and Laura first approached me about this second edition, I was pretty skeptical and reluctant—that is, until I saw what a good editor and collaborator Laura was when she sent me a sample first chapter. Laura Carroll, an outstanding editor, who is also an expert on overpopulation and author of the well-regarded books, *Families of Two* and *The Baby Matrix,* took her editorial hand to the first *Man Swarm* and led the second edition project. I am grateful for the great collaborative editorial relationship she and I had throughout the project.

So, thanks much, Laura and David, for having the enthusiasm about *Man Swarm* to see it as a way to reach another audience and for having the motivation and skill to make it happen.

I'd also like to thank Laura's team—Derek Murphy, who designed the cover, proofreader Amanda Brown, and Lisa DeSpain, who formatted this edition for soft cover and eBook versions.

In my view, there is no better funder in the conservation fellowship than the Weeden Family Foundation, directed by my friend Don Weeden. The Weeden Family Foundation is one of the few conservation foundations that has not fallen to political correctness and turned its back on overpopulation issues. Those at this foundation well understand that the Man swarm underlies all our conservation plights and that we must deal with it if we are to have hope for long-term success on the horde of conservation emergencies before us. Don Weeden is one of the great conservation leaders of his time. He and the Weeden Foundation stepped up to be the main underwriter of this second edition of the *Man Swarm* project.

I write or do little without asking a troika of conservation friends to give me advice: Susan Morgan, John Davis, and Christianne Hinks. They were deeply involved in the first edition and continued to advise me on this second one as well. John reviewed the new manuscript with his keen eye.

This second edition of *Man Swarm* is dedicated, like the first edition, to one of my heroes, Hugh Iltis. Professor Iltis is one of the world's great botanists, the longtime director of the University of Wisconsin-Madison herbarium, and one of the first biologists to clearly see that we were causing a mass extinction. He has grounded this Sixth Great Extinction in five hundred million years to the Man swarm. Since I first met Hugh, he has been my mentor for overpopulation and the reason I swore over ten years ago to put overpopulation at the core of my conservation message. Thank you, Hugh, you've inspired me (as well as many others) more than you know.

Finally, I thank all of you who read this book and make the commitment to do something to solve the overpopulation problem. You are the true heroes.

Dave Foreman
Sheenjek River, Arctic National Wildlife Refuge, Alaska,
July 2014

ABOUT DAVE FOREMAN & LAURA CARROLL

Dave Foreman

Dave Foreman has been one of North America's leading conservationists for over the last forty years.

His work in wilderness protection began in the 1970s, when he served as Southwest Regional Representative and the Director of Wilderness Affairs for The Wilderness Society. In the '70s, he also served as a board member for the New Mexico chapter of The Nature Conservancy.

In the 1980s, Dave co-founded and led the environmental advocacy group, Earth First! which focuses on front-line, direct action approach to protecting wilderness. From 1982 to 1988, he also served as editor of the *Earth First! Journal*.

In 1990s, he co-founded the Wildlands Project (now The Wildlands Network), which continues its work on establishing a network of protected wilderness areas across North America. Dave co-founded the *Wild Earth Journal*, which is now the official periodical for The Wildlands Network. From 1995 to 1997 he served on the Sierra Club's board of directors, and in 1997 he co-founded New Mexico Wilderness Alliance.

In 2003, Dave and the board of directors of the Wildlands Project founded The Rewilding Institute, a nonprofit organization dedicated to "the development and promotion of ideas and strategies to advance continental-scale conservation in North America" and to a hopeful vision for the future of wild nature and human civilization in North America.

Today he continues to play an integral role at The Rewilding Institute and in addition to writing books, is a sought after speaker on rewilding, wilderness, wildlife, and overpopulation issues.

He has canoed and rafted some of the wildest rivers in North America, is a hiker, backpacker, birder, and photographer. He lives in his hometown of Albuquerque, New Mexico, with his wife, Nancy Morton, who is a nurse, and their two cats, Gila and Blue.

In addition to the second edition of *Man Swarm: How Overpopulation is Killing the Wild World*, Dave Foreman's books include:

Man Swarm and the Killing of Wildlife (First Edition)

Take Back Conservation

Rewilding North America: A Vision for Conservation in the 21ˢᵗ Century

Confessions of an Eco-Warrior

The Big Outside: Descriptive Inventory of the Big Wilderness Areas of the United States

The Lobo Outback Funeral Home

Laura Carroll

Since 2000, Laura Carroll has worked as a freelance editor and nonfiction writer. She has used her editorial savvy to assist writers, businesses, and professionals in private and non-profit sectors in reaching their communications goals.

Earlier in her career Laura worked in business psychology and as a trial consultant. She has worked with many organizations on human resource and communications effectiveness and assisted trial lawyers with case strategy, pre-trial research, witness preparation, and jury selection on high profile civil cases.

Laura also writes nonfiction. Laura is the author of *Families of Two: Interviews With Happily Married Couples Without Children by Choice*, which received international acclaim and paved the way for her to become an expert and leading voice on the childfree choice. Her latest book is *The Baby Matrix: Why Freeing Our Minds From Outmoded Thinking About Parenthood & Reproduction Will Create a Better World*. She is also the author of *Finding Fulfillment From the Inside Out*, which has been used in college life planning courses.

Laura is a seasoned leader of personal and professional development seminars, has appeared on a variety of television shows, including *Good Morning America* and *The Early Show*, and has been featured on national radio, in print and digital media to discuss social science topics.

In the process of writing *The Baby Matrix*, Laura budded as an overpopulation activist. This led her to become passionate about bringing *Man Swarm* to a larger audience as a way for more people to learn about the overpopulation crisis and to be inspired to action to help solve it.

ABOUT THE REWILDING INSTITUTE

Mission

To develop and promote the ideas and strategies to advance continental-scale conservation in North America, particularly the need for large carnivores and a permeable landscape for their movement and to offer a bold, scientifically-credible, practically achievable, and hopeful vision for the future of wild Nature and human civilization in North America.

It pursues this mission by means of:

❖ Its website: http://rewilding.org. The website provides information about the integration of traditional wildlife and wildlands conservation with conservation biology to advance landscape-scale conservation. The site gives explanations of key concepts with downloadable documents and links to important papers, essential books, and many groups working on various continental-scale conservation initiatives in North America.

❖ *Around the Campfire* with Dave Foreman, an internet conservation column on policy, ethics, and lore. Subscribe at: http://rewilding.org/rewildit/about-tri/about-dave-foremans-around-the-campfire/.

❖ Lectures and seminars by Dave Foreman for colleges, nonprofit groups, conservation conferences, zoos, and museums. To set up a talk, contact http://rewilding.org/rewildit/contact-us/.

❖ The publishing of the series, *For the Wild Things* by Dave Foreman, for which *Man Swarm and the Killing of Wildlife* and *Take Back Conservation* are a part.

❖ Working through sundry means for a strong North American Wildlands Network with at least four Continental Wildways and bringing back native wildlife to suitable habitat.

The bedrock of The Rewilding Institute is to fight the Sixth Great Extinction, which is now going on and driven wholly by one species—Us.

Made in the USA
San Bernardino, CA
06 March 2015